"In my world—advertising—
the Super Bowl is judgment
day. If politicians have
Election Day and Hollywood
has the Oscars, advertising
has the Super Bowl."

—Jerry Della Femina
writing in *The Wall Street Journal*

"Super Bowl Sunday is all about commotion. Ads that contribute to the din are at a disadvantage versus the ones that draw the story out and the viewer in."

—Bob Garfield,
in "Bob Garfield's Ad Review," *Advertising Age*

THE SUPER BOWL OF ADVERTISING

THE SUPER BOWL OF ADVERTISING

How the Commercials Won the Game

BY BERNICE KANNER

Foreword by
Ted Sann and Phil Dusenberry

Bloomberg PRESS

PRINCETON

First edition published 2004
1 3 5 7 9 10 8 6 4 2

Library of Congress Cataloging-in-Publication Data

Kanner, Bernice.
    The Super Bowl of advertising : how the commercials won the game / Bernice Kanner ; foreword by Ted Sann and Phil Dusenberry.
            p. cm.
Includes index.
    ISBN 1-57660-131-5 (alk. paper)
    1. Television advertising—United States—History. 2. Super Bowl. I. Title.

    HF6146. T42K363 2003
    659.14'3'0973—dc21   2003052212

Acquiring editor: JARED KIELING
Book design: BARBARA DIEZ GOLDENBERG

CONTENTS

ACKNOWLEDGMENTS

THERE'S A GREAT DEAL MORE historical information about the teams and players who appeared on the Super Bowl than about those in the back rooms crafting the other Super Bowl. Unearthing information about those early advertisers in particular was a Herculean task borne cheerfully and energetically by legions of agency staffers, client teams, and production crews—so many, in fact, that to cite them individually would require an appendix. For those who have aided by providing details, confirmations, or clearances for art I offer a sincere and boundless thank you.

Yet I do want to single out for special appreciation creative doyens Phil Dusenberry, formerly chairman of BBDO North America, and Ted Sann, currently chairman of BBDO New York and vice chairman, BBDO North America, not just for creating the foreword for the book but for creating so many of the memorable Super Bowl commercials that made the game an advertising showcase, and, of course, for providing me with access and assistance in the planning and development of this book.

If a project can have a guardian angel, this one's was June Baloutine, senior vice president and director of creative operations at BBDO. Because of her insights, intelligence, and persistence as well as that of her teammates, Norma Bucknor, Jaime Tanaka, and Ryan Woodring, the pages crackle with visual excitement. And deep gratitude to Sylvia Wachtel, chief of BBDO Information Resources, and her team Christina Rawlins and Renee Dichiara, as well as

Janna Delgado in creative and Ed Connor in production, and to the American Association of Advertising Agencies library staff for accommodating my many requests. A special thanks to communications director Roy Elvove. Many thanks also to the team at Pinder Lane, including Bob Thixton and Dick Duane, who helped in securing art permissions.

ON THE BLOOMBERG SIDE, it was editorial director Jared Kieling who held up the firmament of this book with grace and courtesy, through dark times. More than an overseer, he was a reluctant accomplice, in the trenches every step. This book is as much his work as my own. It is also the result of tremendously talented efforts from editors Janet Bamford, herself an author, and associate editor Tracy Tait, whose intimate knowledge of the book as it took shape kept everyone who was involved safely on top of a continually shifting mountain of images, text, and details.

Bloomberg Press's managing editor and creative director Barbara Diez Goldenberg oversaw the layout and editorial production of the book with her team of designers and production editors, JoAnne Kanaval, Mary Macher, and Maris Williams, with prepress and quality control help from George Mahlberg, Marcia Matrisciano, Gerry Burke, and Chris Bartels. To them all, enormous thanks.

Senior editor Christine Miles helped coordinate text and captions and provided many useful ideas along the way, senior editor Ellen Cannon checked proofs under very tight deadlines, and Priscilla Treadwell, director of subsidiary rights, stepped in to arrange some much-needed clearances. And, of course, thank you, thank you, thank you to John Crutcher, publisher of Bloomberg Press, who oversaw the sales and publicity efforts for the book, and to Bill Inman, editor-in-chief of Bloomberg Publishing, and David Wachtel, director of media for Bloomberg L.P., for their insightful collusion.

AND AS ALWAYS, immeasurable love to my wonderful, supportive family, husband David Cuming, and son and daughter Andrew and Elisabeth, who bore witness to the birth of this elephant.

"Not only are you gathering people around the set to watch your message in great numbers, but there's a shelf life to advertising on the Super Bowl which goes beyond the game."

—Phil Dusenberry

"It's all about confidence in your creative and confidence in your message. When you have that confidence, the Super Bowl is a great place to be. Otherwise, there are a lot of reasons for not being there."

—Ted Sann

FOREWORD

IN THE OLD MOVIES ABOUT BROADWAY, when the curtain went down, the troupe always headed for Sardi's to wait for the opening-night reviews. Some kid in a waiter's uniform would come running in with a dozen copies of the *Herald Tribune*, and everyone would rifle the pages looking for the write-up. The reviews were always raves.

Most of the year, "review" is a dirty word in the ad business. If an account is in review, it means you're inches away from losing it to another agency. But once a year, the ad biz and show biz converge for the Super Bowl, and we get overnight reviews, just like old George S. Kaufman used to.

Seconds after the final whistle, we retreat to CyberSardi's and check out how our ads did on the various Internet opinion polls. Even a couple of jaded, been-there-done-that ad guys like us revel in the excitement. There it is in black and white. They loved that one, they hated that one, and, uh-oh, they ignored that one. The Super Bowl is as close as ad people get to opening night.

Most of the time we're judged by metrics and testing and client opinions, but this one time, the critics and the public tell us what they love and hate.

The Super Bowl, in a word, is *it*. The big one. The ad show of shows. When it comes to launching new campaigns and introducing new ads, nothing, but nothing, comes close to that one dazzling day in January.

First, the TV audience is double the size of that for any other TV event. And second, this is no regular audience. This audience is *primed to watch the commercials.* This is the one day of the year on which viewers all across America actually look forward to the spots. It's estimated that only half the people watching are actual football fans. The rest are there for the beer, the chips, the party, and to see the ads.

So for advertising people, it's the rarest of moments: being in front of *an audience actually willing to be advertised to.* But you'd better not show anybody a cutaway drawing of a sinus cavity or any flaming metaphors for hemorrhoid discomfort, because they'll zap you to ad oblivion.

The Super Bowl audience is ready and willing to absorb your brand message as long as the ad gives something back, as long as it entertains. A great Super Bowl ad can't lecture, it can't cajole; it has to win the hearts and minds of the viewers with its wit, its charm, and its outright uniqueness.

For seasoned Super Bowl ad veterans, there's no mystery to this. It's rooted in the simple reason people watch TV in the first place: entertainment.

That's what the great Super Bowl commercials are all about—full-scale entertainment packed into miraculous 30- and 60-second packages that deliver a real brand message. The big payout is famous, engaging, from-the-heart messages that can add huge value to a client's brands.

The fact is, the truly superb Super Bowl spots entertain, but they also sell like hell.

Apple's "1984" catapulted Macintosh to immediate fame and relative fortune.

Two-thirds of Master Lock's entire annual ad budget played out in a single Super Bowl spot that turned a nowhere brand into a household name. Go ahead, name another lock.

And a brand close to the hearts of every BBDOer, Pepsi, gave the competition at Coke sleepless nights with knockout spots that boosted sales and won *USA Today*'s Super Bowl Ad Meter survey six times.

So it's no wonder advertisers are spending small fortunes on the game, not just for media space, but on TV production as well, and for big-ticket celebrity endorsers who add yet more glitter to this lustrous event, from Michael Jordan to Jackie Chan to the Osbournes.

Like many top advertisers, Pepsi swears by the Super Bowl. And so does Visa, FedEx, Frito-Lay, M&M's, Nike, Budweiser, and many more.

And, for the right clients, so does BBDO.

For creative people—the people who make the ads—the Super Bowl has all the pressure, all the competitive angst, of the game itself. Reputations, legends, and careers have been made—or broken—on Super Bowl spots. The pressure to be the best is overwhelming. And the process of getting a spot to the big game has all the rigors and hard knocks of the regular football season.

The Super Bowl ad season starts early. Agency creatives are in the trenches as early as June, drumming up concepts and executions that won't debut for another six or seven months.

Hundreds of ideas spill out of word processors and layout pads all across the country. But only a select few will make the cut. At BBDO, the "kill rate" is exceptionally high.

It's those surviving fifty or so spots that will be presented in all their glory in the largest one-day sale in history. No other media vehicle commands as much money as a spot on The Game, because no other vehicle gives a brand such incredible reach, ratings, and impact.

A spot on Super Bowl Sunday—just one—makes a huge public statement. It says you're part of a special culture. It says you've arrived. But while just "being there" worked for Chauncey Gardiner, it won't work for just any old ad. You've got to spin some magic. And that's what separates the real players, the all-stars, from the rest of the league.

So while we're writing this, we're busy getting ready for next year's game. What are you going to see? We have no idea—we can only tell you that the ones you'll remember will be big, enthralling, and talked about for weeks after you've forgotten the score of the game.

TED SANN
Chairman, Chief Creative Officer
BBDO New York

PHIL DUSENBERRY
Former Chairman
BBDO North America

Within just a few years after the first Super Bowl in 1967, the televised game became a national ritual. Today, one viewer in ten tunes in just for the ads.

INTRODUCTION

THE NATIONAL FOOTBALL LEAGUE'S Super Bowl is not just the crowning glory of American football. It is the Super Bowl of advertising, the most watched, most anticipated, most expensive, most influential arena for major-league television advertising. For corporate America, the real event starts when an advertiser makes its pitch for a piece of your wallet.

It is *the* place for advertisers to be seen and to showcase their best, and for 750 million viewers worldwide to watch. Eight of the eleven most watched programs in U.S. TV history were Super Bowls.

Each year four out of ten U.S. households hunker down to eye the big game. There's ample opportunity to see the ads: In a typical game, the football moves for just eighteen minutes, yet the show takes three hours.

Although it's been dubbed "the sweat lodge of modern masculinity," the Super Bowl audience is a melting pot of every demographic and psychographic group in the country. "It's the one time of year when football fanatics and the sports-challenged commingle in relative peace," says Michael Patti, former vice chairman of advertising agency BBDO. Three out of four members of the audience aren't the traditional male, die-hard football fans, but neophytes of both sexes.

Since it began in 1967, the game has grown to mythic proportions. Thirty thousand seats remained empty in the Los Angeles Coliseum for the inaugural game between the Green Bay Packers and the Kansas City Chiefs. Tickets sold for $6 to $12. Today, the average ticket goes for almost $400. Costs for the ads have followed the same steep trajectory. Ads on Super Bowl I, broadcast by two networks, cost one-fortieth the price of those that ran during XXXIV (2000). While no one actually pays retail—that would be like buying a car for the sticker price—it's still more than $2 million for 30 seconds.

Baseball, hockey, and basketball all have their best-of-seven contests to crown a champ. But professional football settles things in one game— and funnels all of the excitement, interest, and hype into that game. More than any other sports championship, this media event is a cultural experience as well as a mirror of popular culture. Lawrence Wenner, a professor of communication at the University of San Francisco, says that, fueled as it is by mass advertising and sports mania—"two super-charged engines of modern life"—Super Sunday has become "a cultural high holy day," a ritualized gathering of family and friends to bid farewell to winter and welcome spring. Indeed, "If Jesus were alive today, he'd be at the Super Bowl," Norman Vincent Peale once proclaimed. The promotions start long before the first set of downs, when other sports, along with the TV and film industries, are relatively quiet. There are Super Bowl sales, specials, recipes. Sports analysts talk the game to death before kickoff and perform endless postmortems after the final whistle.

It's an even bigger at-home party occasion than New Year's Eve (on average, each Super Bowl party hosts seventeen people), and the only day on which people eat more is Thanksgiving. On average, 6 percent of American workers call in sick on the Monday after.

The Super Bowl has become the stuff of legends. One such: In 1984, the Salt Lake City water systems shut down from an unheard-of amount of simultaneous toilet flushing at halftime. (Actually, a broken water main caused the problem.) Word is that there's no wait at the popular Space Mountain rides during the game because the Disney parks are virtually deserted. (In fact, they're almost as populated as on any other Sunday in January.) Another myth: Two-thirds of all avocados bought in a given year wind up in Super Bowl guacamole. (It's really about 5 percent, roughly half of what it is for Cinco de Mayo.)

What is true is that party-goers consume 14,500 tons of chips and more alcohol than on any day other than New Year's Day and St. Patrick's Day. One in four workers bets in an office pool. During Super Bowl week, sales of large-screen TVs increase fivefold, but it's the slowest weekend for weddings.

There's even a Super Bowl Wall Street predictor. If a team with roots in the old NFL wins, the stock market will climb. If the victor's roots are in the defunct American Football League, stocks will tumble. As ludicrous as it sounds, it's been wrong only seven times in thirty-six years.

While the game is still played by overpaid athletes bulked up to comic proportions, the ads—which were once the same ones the sponsors ran in their regular rotation—are now more often art itself, custom-tailored for the event. Indeed, says Monster.com CEO Jeff Taylor, on this day the "advertising is the program."

The marketing has become so much a part of the Super Bowl that entire portions of the show have been sold off and renamed: In 2000 there was the Charles Schwab & Co. pre-kickoff, the E*Trade halftime show, and the Pontiac postgame cool-down. And, of course, the game is often played in a corporate-named arena, such as the Raymond James Stadium in Tampa, Florida.

By industry calculations, more than two out of three viewers pay attention to the commercials, and more than half talk about them the next day. More than one in ten tune in *just* for the ads, which often cost millions of dollars to produce and air. Commercials on this day are so hotly anticipated that they actually *increase* the size of the audience. Indeed, it may be the only time when people talk about the ads *before* the event. Spots are often released ahead of time to the media, as political ads are, and after the game, some newspapers survey readers to see what resonated. CBS has even run a "Super Bowl's Greatest Commercial" show in some years. "For one day a year, advertising becomes a friend rather than a party-crasher," says Michael Suissa, chairman of Suissa Miller Advertising. For ad agencies and their clients, Super Bowl Sunday is judgment day, says Bob Scarpelli, chief creative officer at DDB Needham. "It represents the grandest prize, the opportunity for a public pat on the back. It's the one day when the pressure to look good is all-consuming." Adds Goodby, Silverstein co-chief Jeff Goodby, "For us ad guys, it's our one chance to make a diving catch in the end zone."

Apple Computer's renowned "1984" spot (see Chapter 2) launched the era when Super Bowl ads became their own separate spectacle. At the time, "having your own computer was like having your own cruise missile," recalled Steve Hayden, now vice chairman of Ogilvy & Mather, who wrote the commercial and claims he's "been riding on the fumes of that ad ever since."

Since then, marketers have seized this venue to introduce new campaigns or products or to take on new names or purposes, and the commercials have acquired lives of their own. Some are disappointingly mundane, but most are creative, funny, witty, and emotionally arousing—often better entertainment, minute-for-minute, than what's happening on the field.

Not every type of advertising works in this venue. For years, mainly well-known and fat-walleted marketers ventured into this stadium. But small-timers like Master Lock and Mail Boxes Etc. also scored by making it part of their game plan. Ad industry wisdom holds that this arena works best for established brands and as part of a campaign, not a one-shot. Increasingly, tie-ins are lined up to pay off before the first kick—and after the last.

Beyond building or repositioning brands, launching new products, or trying for a toehold in an emerging market, Super Bowl ads are about motivating the sales team and distributors and making a public splash. "Running on the Super Bowl says we've arrived," says Don Moonjian, vice president of advertising at Alamo Rent A Car.

A single Super Bowl commercial can change our vocabulary (Whassup?!), sense of humor (money coming out the wazoo), buying traditions (Sensor razors, M&M's), or product associations (Reebok shook its women's shoe mantle here).

Viewers still glimpse some tract houses amidst what has become TV's ritziest beachfront property, but those are, for the most part, from local "spot" market buyers. Take Hair Club for Men ads on local stations: They show women fawning over a "club" member, or a hirsute guy gloating over a balding rival.

Some experts claim that because the games themselves are filled with conflict and suspense, the ads that work best break that tension. Others say that the more fantastic, special-effects laden, campy, the more chockablock with celebs, the more "out there" an ad is, the better. BBDO, which traditionally has so many commercials in the game that the Super Bowl has been nicknamed the BBDO Bowl, has a formula: tickle the funny bone, tug at the heartstrings, and toss in a surprise ending. Tactics can include celebrities, kids, animals, Michael Jordan, and product as hero—or none of the above. "The increasing boredom of the game has put added pressure on advertisers to be entertaining," says retired chairman Phil Dusenberry.

"Long, detailed, rational product messages don't do well in this three-hour escape where people want to be grabbed quickly, and get something back for watching," says BBDO chairman and creative chief Ted Sann. "You need to show, more than tell, a story. During the big game, ads that depend on visual puns tend to succeed." Spots that ask you to think about your mortgage, sniffles, or job generally don't work.

Ads tend to be more heart-racing than heartwarming. For every regal Clydesdale pulling the Budweiser wagon, there are ten splattered frogs. "Humor has replaced sentiment in making the needle move here," says Dusenberry. Humor works because the Super Bowl is one of the rare occasions when TV is watched by groups, notes adman Jerry Della Femina. "The audience isn't in the mood for warm-and-fuzzy. Save that for the Olympics."

As a communal national ritual that everyone watches and knows everyone else is watching, the Super Bowl is a reservoir of emotional and symbolic patriotic content. NASA and the NFL have been aligned since SB III, when the Apollo 8 astronauts led a pregame pledge of allegiance. During the Cold War, the Super Bowl was viewed as "a bastion against world communism and the counterculture and all the perceived ills of American society," says Mike Oriard, who wrote the 2001 book *King Football*.

During the Vietnam War, Richard Nixon initiated the ritual of the presidential postgame phone call to the victorious coach. On January 25, 1981, the New Orleans Superdome sported a massive yellow ribbon as a salute to the American hostages released by Iran five days before. A decade later, Whitney Houston's rendition of the national anthem was followed by a flyover of military jets. Just as manufacturers use red, white, and blue to legitimize their products during the year, the NFL, TV networks, and sponsors use patriotism to legitimize the Super Bowl as part of the American experience, says University of Colorado sociologist Jay Coakley.

The Super Bowl is particularly effective for products that need to generate widespread common knowledge and acceptance—like the Discover credit card in 1986, says UCLA economist Michael Suk-Young Chwe. And it scores well for products like cars, sneakers, and soda that thrive on widely understood brand associations.

The venue is not without detractors. Advertisers routinely rail against the clutter and the exorbitant prices the networks charge, and they point to alternatives like the Academy Awards (a/k/a the "Super Bowl for Women") and the Olympics. Former Bozell Worldwide creative chief Jay Schulberg calls this "an extravagant exercise in folly" which "forgets that advertising's purpose is to create a selling message that stays with you long after the last touchdown."

Some marketers deem this "Ego Bowl" delusionary. "They're not targeting consumers as much as each other," says Harvard professor Stephen Greyser. Compared with the Internet or targeted niche approaches, this old-fashioned big-tent carnival of commercialism is viewed by some as a dinosaur.

At $20,000-a-blink rates, you could buy half a dozen prime-time spots for the cost of one on Super Sunday and still have money left to sponsor hours on late-night cable, some argue. "It's the most expensive empty room that you can broadcast to," says Dave Stewart, professor of marketing at the University of Southern California. When the ads roll on, viewers head for the kitchen or bathroom. Those who stay put at Super Bowl parties are probably gabbing about the game—not focusing on the ads, he adds. John Hancock Mutual Life Insurance stopped sponsoring the game because, said chief David D'Alessandro, "There's probably not another event with more people watching and fewer people paying attention."

Despite the critics, many advertisers concede the Super Bowl is still *the* premier play for talking to an audience of this size and quality—more efficient than the big miniseries, an NCAA Championship game, or the Oscars. The day-after recall of Super Bowl ads is 52 percent, versus 23 percent for the average prime-time commercial. And ad agency Cramer-Krasselt found most viewers liked Super Bowl ads more than ads in general.

Marketers go the whole nine yards to get here in large part precisely *because* its price tag of $2 million for 30 seconds towers over the $400,000 that the top-rated series shows get. As the highest-rated prime-time series of a recent season, *Friends* had a 15 rating; that year the Super Bowl had a 40.4.

"Where else can you reach half the people in the U.S. at once?" asks Hal Riney & Partners executive Doug Sealy. "Mathematically, the cost [roughly $9 per thousand viewers] makes good sense. Emotionally, it makes better sense. An ad gets noticed and remembered here. It gets hyped. It not only has a great benefit emotionally, but down the road it creates profits."

Even with its bloated cost, the Bowl is still a relative bargain, says Joel Segal, EVP of national broadcasting for McCann-Erickson. "There's a certain magic, a rub-off . . . that you can't get from any other program, especially if you build a promotion around it. No other event has this kind of cachet, so it doesn't fit within normal media strategies."

It's not an investment made for purely rational or objective reasons, says David Verklin, CEO of Carat USA. Purely from a media perspective, the divisional playoffs are a far better value. "Rather, it's purchased for its ability to reach a huge, unduplicated swath of the American consuming public. In many ways it's about the intangibles."

Advertising in the "one big TV tent that hasn't collapsed puts you in the spotlight," says legendary adman George Lois. "If you aren't running a great commercial, everybody's taking shots at you. But if it's a good-to-great commercial, it's a great coup."

This book is the tale of some of these coups and a sketch of that advertising evolution—noting the triumphs and embarrassing flops, along with some ads you never saw. Not all of the thousands of commercials that ran on the Super Bowl are cited here. This is not a yearbook or complete compendium that charts this history. Rather, it's an exploration of highlights and lowlights, and a look at some ads that are significant in some way—because they broke new ground; represented a major campaign, movement, or milestone; or reflected life at the time in a unique way.

There's a residual halo effect to much of the advertising described here, a great water-cooler extension to what aired. There is tangible merchandising value associated with such a long-lasting afterlife. People rerun the ads in their minds and in their conversations long after the show.

It is, after all, not the moderately good bowl. It is the Super Bowl.

THE SUPER BOWLS

I	1967	XXIII	1989
II	1968	XXIV	1990
III	1969	XXV	1991
IV	1970	XXVI	1992
V	1971	XXVII	1993
VI	1972	XXVIII	1994
VII	1973	XXIX	1995
VIII	1974	XXX	1996
IX	1975	XXXI	1997
X	1976	XXXII	1998
XI	1977	XXXIII	1999
XII	1978	XXXIV	2000
XIII	1979	XXXV	2001
XIV	1980	XXXVI	2002
XV	1981	XXXVII	2003
XVI	1982	XXXVIII	2004
XVII	1983	XXXIX	2005
XVIII	1984	XL	2006
XIX	1985	XLI	2007
XX	1986	XLII	2008
XXI	1987	XLIII	2009
XXII	1988	XLIV	2010

PART ONE

THE BIG PICTURE

In 1967, LBJ was pacing in the White House, the generation gap was a chasm, and no one had any idea what a cultural institution the Super Bowl was about to become.

1

IN THE BEGINNING

ALTHOUGH IT AIRED on both CBS and NBC, neither network has a tape. Neither does the National Football League, nor the victorious Green Bay Packers. New York's Museum of Television and Radio has only the audio track from NBC. But even that recording conveys how right from the beginning on January 15, 1967, the bowl of bowls between the feuding National and American Football Leagues demonstrated a fledgling merchandising cachet. Today the game has grown into an institutional magnet drawing more than 130 million Americans and 750 million viewers worldwide.

Before advertising's creative revolution of the 1970s, before Apple's 1984 big bang, what sponsored the first game already mattered just as much as what happened in it. Seen from an armchair thirty-five years in the future, the commercials seem awkward, amateurish, and interminable (sixty seconds was the norm; today it's fifteen or thirty). Few commercials debuted during the first Super Bowl. Nonetheless, they carried considerable clout. A Winston cigarette commercial on NBC that was still running when action resumed after halftime prompted the refs to whistle the opening kick dead. Packers coach Vince Lombardi fumed while his team was forced to kick again.

Originally billed as the World Championship game, the Super Bowl was created in 1966 as part of the merger agreement between the National Football

Haggar
will be big
on College All-Stars vs.
Green Bay Packers
on ABC-TV

HAGGAR
'67

All
America
will see new
Haggar Mustang
and Forever Prest
slacks (50% Acrilan®
acrylic-50% Avril® rayon
and acetate) on the coast-
to-coast telecast of the
Green Bay Packers vs.
College All-Stars August 4.
Also weekly in August on
ABC-TV's "Wide World
of Sports." It's the
kickoff for your biggest
back-to-school and
back-to-fall sales.

HAGGAR
Slacks

Cash in on slacks' biggest year with slacks' biggest name.

HAGGAR PRINT AD Haggar promised its pants would stay fresh-pressed through heat and humidity. The company continued using the football motif in a 1967 mailing.

League and the then eight-year-old American Football League. Beginning in January 1967, the two league champions would meet each year in a title game. Lamar Hunt, architect of the AFL, owner of the Kansas City Chiefs, and one of six committeemen entrusted to orchestrate the merger, was musing about his daughter playing with a "Super Ball" that took crazy bounces when he blurted out the name. NFL Commissioner Pete Rozelle thought it hokey and presumptuous. "Super Bowl" did not appear on the cover of a program until 1969. It was the media that christened the day of the game as Super Sunday.

Some 63,000 fans watched from Los Angeles's 92,000-seat Memorial Coliseum as the Packers pocketed the first game, 35–10, from the AFL's Chiefs. In an attempt to fill seats, broadcasters considered a local TV blackout, but protests dissuaded them from the plan. It was the only Super Bowl that didn't sell out.

Another 60 million fans watched on TV (dwarfing the prior record for a single sports event, a 1963 Yankees versus Dodgers World Series game). This inaugural audience was split between two networks by a decree by commissioner Rozelle. Eighteen million people caught the game on the radio.

NBC had asked $75,000 for a one-minute commercial; CBS, $85,000. (That's 900 percent less in constant dollars than a spot sells for on the game now.) A few weeks before kickoff, Ford had balked at the price but relented after a minor discount was granted. By January 1, every spot had been snapped up. As the game drew near, CBS and NBC waged intense promotional campaigns. More than ego was on the line: Audience dominance would help lure sponsors for the next season and allow them to push up the rates. On CBS, three of every four of its promotions after January 1 focused on Super Sunday. NBC began running "crawls," the moving text at the bottom of the TV screen, in December. Instead of ending on D-Day, the hoopla seemed to intensify after the game. CBS gloated in a full-page *New York Times* ad the next day that it had won the network battle. Many advertisers—including Chrysler, RCA, RJ Reynolds Tobacco, McDonald's, and Lorillard—had bought time on both. Their target was the Archie Bunker man, back in the days when men were men.

"THE ONE BEER" Schaefer called itself "the one beer to have when you're having more than one."

In promoting its acrylic and rayon slacks that "just fit better naturally," Haggar tried to sell men on physical and mental comfort. McDonald's boasted of selling "hundreds of thousands of burgers every day," then touted its ingredients. And Goodyear played to men's chivalry, offering up a damsel in distress. "The loneliest place in the world is any place a lady has a flat," a man asserted. That's why Goodyear developed the Double Edge, "a tire that could keep on going—that could keep the steering wheel from jerking out of her hands." In a

high-energy musical, the "good guys" at Chrysler urged viewers to "nail down the deal of the century on a Dodge Coronet 440" or follow their hearts to the first annual Plymouth Dealers Win-You-Over-Sale. American Airlines touted smooth flying via a new "special computer programmed for wind and temperature" on every plane. Winston and Salem cigarettes were there. Schaefer continued its five-year-old positioning as "the one beer to have."

TAREYTON PRINT CAMPAIGN In a print ad that echoed their Super Bowl spot, Tareyton's team would rather fight than switch.

"JUST PLAIN WAITING" Anheuser-Busch revealed the secret ingredient in brewing its Busch beer—old-fashioned patience while the beer forms its own natural bubbles.

Ford built a massive Masonite duplicate of *Motor Trend* magazine's Car of the Year award in the Mojave Desert. Cameras in helicopters followed a real cougar perched atop a new Mercury as it moved onto the huge medallion, while twenty other cars encircled it.

Eastern Airlines's "The Wings of Man" celebrated the miracle of flight and showed happy people reuniting. American Tobacco's Tareyton team vowed they'd "rather fight than switch." Liggett & Myers plugged Lark's gas-trap filter. And President Johnson reminded Americans of their patriotic duty to buy U.S. Savings Bonds to support troops in Vietnam.

Super Bowl II (1968) seemed like a rerun with the Packers, this time beating the Oakland Raiders, 33–14. A technical glitch caused almost 80 percent of television sets to go dark for a few minutes in the first half. A Newport cigarette commercial that aired then was rerun later in the game, giving Lorillard a valuable "make-good."

Many original advertisers returned. Metropolitan Life and Winston ran catchy jingles: "We're helping more than forty million people who know the future is now" and "Winston tastes good like a cigarette should." Salem was back to "refresh your taste." United Airlines told business fliers to bring their wives.

TWA said it with music—Jimmy Webb's "Up, Up and Away." Chrysler Plymouth borrowed Petula Clark's recording of "The Beat Goes On," to synchronize with headlights flashing and horns tooting. And Goodyear doctored the Nancy Sinatra hit, "These Boots Are Made for Walking," to say its tires are "made for rolling, because Goodyear built them to."

IN 1969, THE NATIONAL ASSOCIATION OF BROADCASTERS increased its scrutiny of violence in TV programming, PBS launched *Sesame Street,* and Neil Armstrong took mankind's first step on the moon. But before all that, on January 12, 1969, in Super Bowl III, New York Jets quarterback Joe Namath made good on his promise—no, guarantee—to defeat the favored Baltimore Colts in Miami's

Orange Bowl stadium. After "Broadway Joe's" triumph, he became a folk hero, the Super Bowl became an established monument, and the AFL became a contender.

Weeks before, advertisers had bought eighteen minutes (at $135,000 each) in the game along with four minutes (at $50,000 each) in the pregame. MetLife bought four in the postgame show at $65,000 each. The normal prime-time tariff then was $46,000 for 60 seconds. With antismoking sentiment erupting, Lorillard bailed, but RJR quickly grabbed its two minutes.

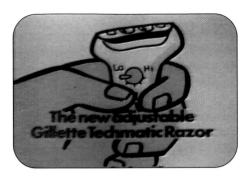

TECHMATIC'S CARTOON
Gillette introduced the new Techmatic Razor as the younger brother of its old Techmatic for average beards.

Some ads were literally cartoons. Gillette's new adjustable Techmatic razor "for light, average, and heavy beards" appeared in an animation. A Road Runner cartoon character guided the tour of "what Plymouth's up to now."

Others were unintentionally cartoonish. Men waxed jubilant at discovering sprigs of mint in their Rapid Shave Menthol.

During the 1970s, while the game gained popularity, its advertising remained largely pedestrian. Yet there were flashes of brilliance and daring. During Super Bowl VI on January 16, 1972, while the Dallas Cowboys stampeded over the Miami Dolphins in New Orleans, Coca-Cola was making ad history with music.

Viewers that day saw a veritable United Nations of fresh-faced young people assembled on a hillside singing "I'd like to teach the world to sing, in perfect harmony...I'd like to buy the world a Coke and keep it company." A helicopter-borne camera panned back to reveal a throng of 400. "I'd like to buy the world a home, and furnish it with love; Grow apple trees and honey bees and snow-

"HILLTOP" Coca-Cola made advertising history with its "I'd like to teach the world to sing" message of peace.

"MEAN JOE GREENE" Was it the Coke or the boy's generosity that revived Pittsburgh's Mean Joe? The young fan went home with his idol's jersey.

white turtle doves."

A year earlier, on January 18, 1971, Pan Am flight 12, carrying young McCann-Erickson copywriter and songwriter Bill Backer, had made an unexpected overnight stopover in Ireland due to fog. Backer's ire softened as he watched passengers come together over Cokes. The soda was a social catalyst. Lines of a song floated into his head, and he jotted them on a paper napkin. The next day, in London, he and writer-musicians Billy Davis and Roger Cook crafted a storyboard for one of the most beloved commercials of all time.

Several months later, on a hillside near Rome, young people clad in their national costumes stood in an inverted pyramid, clutching Cokes. Directed in sign language, they sang (okay, lip-synched) a moving tribute to peace, love, and world unity. The 60-second spot cost a then-hefty $225,000 to produce.

"The bottlers felt it didn't sell hard enough," recalls Backer, who then produced a second commercial that embellished the singing. "That's the song I sing...What the world wants today...A song of peace that echoes on... And never goes away."

Many bottlers still had reservations, and panned it as treacly. But when the new version aired experimentally in July, the public lapped it up. Foreign bottlers now clamored for versions in their own languages. South

"STRIPPER" Noxzema's sexy Swede urged men to "take it all off."

Africa asked for one without blacks. (Coke refused.)

Two Top 40 versions, by the New Seekers and the Hillside Singers, sold more than a million copies by 1972. The "Hilltop" campaign ran for six years. (For SB 1990, Coke hired the Pinkerton Agency to find some of the original performers plus their children for a nostalgic sequel on that same Italian hillside.)

As "Hilltop" wound down, Coke was readying another blockbuster: "Mean Joe Greene." The wounded, dispirited Pittsburgh Steeler limps toward the locker room as a shy young fan tries to buck up his idol. Finally, the dejected lad presses his sixteen-ounce Coke on the glowering defensive lineman. Mean Joe relents and chugs it while lyrics erupt: "A Coke and a smile makes me feel good, makes me feel nice." As the crestfallen boy turns to leave, Greene, humanity restored, tosses him his jersey.

Bill Van Loan, then Coke vice president, said the ads featured "product as hero, causing the smile. While Pepsi invited people to join some mythical group, Coke aimed to own the world of smiling Americans." The shoot (in a high school stadium tunnel to emphasize Greene's bulk) took three days, in part because young Tommy Oken kept flubbing his lines, so awed was he by Greene. Copywriter Penny Hawkey wanted an emotional spot, not more happy jingles and well-scrubbed folks working up a thirst. "People responded to its seeming realism and honesty," she said, "and Coke never over-promised." It was merely a pause that refreshes, not an elixir that would change the world.

Coke wasn't alone in harnessing the power of music. Noxzema used music *and* a heaping dollop of sex to sell Medicated Instant Shave Cream with Swedish model Gunilla Knutson bumping and grinding to David Rose's hit instrumental, "The Stripper," teasing men to "Take it off, take it all off" as they shaved. One spot in 1972 starred Joe Namath still basking in his Super Bowl win when costar Farrah Fawcett meets him in the bathroom. "Ladies, want to see Joe Namath get creamed?" she asks cheekily before lathering him up.

"CAMPING" Rodney Dangerfield and John Madden joined Miller Lite's less filling/tastes great debate.

"COWBOYS & INDIANS" Into the 1980s, Miller Brewing Co. had cowboys and Indians continue the debate over whether Miller Lite tastes great or is less filling.

In these still-early days, before Anheuser-Busch had a lock on the game, Miller was buying airtime on every major sport event, leaving Anheuser-Busch to claw for the crumbs. Careful to plug Lite's robust taste and avoid even a whiff of wimpiness, a team at McCann fashioned the "Everything you always wanted in a beer...and less" campaign starring beefy, retired jocks bantering in neighborhood bars over whether it "tastes great" or is "less filling." The first commercial featured Super Bowl hero New York Jet Matt Snell; others used writers Mickey Spillane and Frank Deford, Rodney Dangerfield, football's Deacon Jones and John Madden, baseball's Billy Martin, and basketball's Red Auerbach. "We choose guys you'd love to have a beer with," said Bob Lenz, who conceived the campaign. "We didn't want actors, or superstars, but macho, beery guys who could make fun of themselves."

McDonald's status as the world's most recognized brand in 1996 was at least partly the result of its high-touch ads and its broad appeal. After its spot ran on both networks in Super Bowl III, its store volume jumped 22 percent and McDonald's became a believer.

"CLEAN UP" In this 1971 spot, the "You Deserve a Break Today" anthem established McDonald's as a place moms could bring the family.

Chain founder Ray Kroc used to say that "we're not in the hamburger business; we're in show business." From the start, McDonald's ads aimed for the heart. In addition to the expected "bite and smile" shots, most ads put likable characters in seemingly honest and realistic situations, speaking natural dialogue and filmed in unexpected ways such as extreme close-ups or slow motion. Music is distinctive and mood-enhancing. And there's a little magic moment that surprises you or chokes you up. In 1970, McDonald's was preparing a spot about little islands where you can "get up and get away, to McDonald's." At the last moment they discovered that the island theme was being used elsewhere. So Keith Reinhard, chief of McDonald's ad agency, moved to plan B, playing up the emotional rewards of a McDonald's experience. As an energetic crew cleaned, they sang to music by Barry Manilow.

Then, in 1974, came the tongue twister celebrating the six-year-old Big Mac: Two-all-beef-patties-special-sauce-lettuce-cheese-pickles-onions-on-a-sesame-seed-bun. After an Alabama franchisee ran a promotion awarding free Big Macs to passersby who recited it correctly within four seconds, jingle mania spread. (Those who flubbed it landed in a bloopers commercial.) In rapid succession came "We Do It All for You"; "You, You're the One"; and "Nobody Can Do It Like McDonald's Can"; plus a revival of "You Deserve a Break Today" in 1981.

"HOOK & STALL" In these American Express Travelers Cheques ads starring actor Karl Malden, hapless tourists are victimized by thieves—then chastened by an authority figure incredulous that they hadn't used American Express.

"MONKS" Xerox's monk spot introduced its speedy collating copier.

IN 1974, WHEN ONLY SIX MILLION people carried its green card, American Express suggested empowerment with its now famous "Do you know me?" campaign. High achievers whose names were often better known than their faces would recount an exploit ("I was the first man to climb Mount Everest"), state a problem ("I still forget to change my dollars into dinars before going to Nepal"), then explain why they carry the card ("It's recognized around the world"). At the end, an American Express Card appeared, bearing the name of the famous person.

William Miller, who ran for vice president in 1964 yet still had trouble charging a meal, exclaimed, "Why, with this they treat me as though I'd won." In 1975, voice impressionist Mel Blanc (a/k/a Bugs Bunny) moaned, "They don't care if I'm Daffy Duck. Desthpicable. Without this card the only way I'd get any attention is by saying"—he imitates the stammering Porky Pig— "Th-uh-th-th-That's all, folks."

A concurrent campaign for American Express Travelers Cheques that ran for twenty-one years starred actor Karl Malden, the hard-bitten Detective Lieutenant Mike Stone from *The Streets of San Francisco* TV series. Competition from big banks pushing their own traveler's checks was prompting more people to leave home without American Express. The hard-sell "Don't leave home without them" spots set to ominous music turned its traveler's checks into worldwide currency.

DURING SB XI, on January 9, 1977, the Oakland Raiders smashed the Minnesota Vikings 32–14; the crowd topped 100,000, with another 78 million watching; and Xerox Copiers introduced the world to an engaging monk. Working by candlelight in an austere monastery, a stocky Friar Tuck look-alike painstakingly copies a manuscript. "Ever since people started recording information, there's been a need to duplicate it," says a voice. Brother Dominick gulps when the abbot asks for 500 more copies, then hastens to a local duplicating shop where the owner painlessly runs them off using Xerox's amazing new 9200 Duplicating System. When Brother Dominick presents the 500 sets later that day, his stupefied superior looks heavenward and declares, "It's a miracle."

Allen Kay, then creative director on the account, initially advised Xerox to write to the handful of prospects who could afford the $25,000 machine, but Xerox wanted the world, its employees, and Wall Street to know about the copier. Copywriter Steven Penchina came up with the "It's a miracle" line.

Xerox fretted that it might seem blasphemous. (Religion had not been exploited in ads yet.) New York's Cardinal Cooke blessed it. Huggable Jack Eagle, a 5'4", 210-pound, Jewish, Catskills stand-up comedian, was cast as Brother Dominick because of his pleasant, semi-ethereal look and angelic expression. "Monk" grew "legs," blossomed into a campaign, and ran through 1982.

In Super Bowl XII, the first time the game was played in prime time, Schlitz (Light and Old Milwaukee) made the biggest sports buy in TV history. The Denver Broncos defense—known as "The Orange Crush"—posed for Orange Crush soda wearing "Crush" outfits. Newspapers and magazines packaged their sports sections to tie in with the big TV contest, fueling the hype. The next year, in 1979, UniRoyal named the Steeler tire after the team, then developed an ad campaign around it using the Pittsburgh Steelers as stars.

At the start of the 1980s, the stars were aligned for a conceptual leap—a commercial that could create a new universe for television advertising.

2

1984: THE BIG BANG

GEORGE ORWELL could not have known in 1949, when he depicted a dehumanized totalitarian regime in his gloomy dystopian novel *1984*, that a dark, cinematic commercial sharing its title would hijack his vision.

Apple paid $1 million for the 60-second spot that ran just once—in the 1984 game. But it was repeatedly shown on news programs, and its debut is probably the most publicized moment in advertising history. "1984" helped drive $4.5 million in sales within six hours of its airing and made Chiat/Day a formidable national agency. It launched the genre of advertising as an event and transformed the Super Bowl into an advertising showcase.

The commercial opens with a stark, futuristic vision. Blue-tinted zombies shuffle in lockstep into a massive assembly hall dominated by a huge screen from which Big Brother orates. "For today, we celebrate the first glorious anniversary of the Information Purification Directives. We have created, for the first time in all history ...a garden of pure ideology." The devolved automatons, their heads shaved and mouths agape, sit transfixed while Big Brother drones on: "...where each worker may bloom secure from the pests of contradictory and confusing truths."

Suddenly, an athletic blonde in red shorts bearing the new Mac logo charges

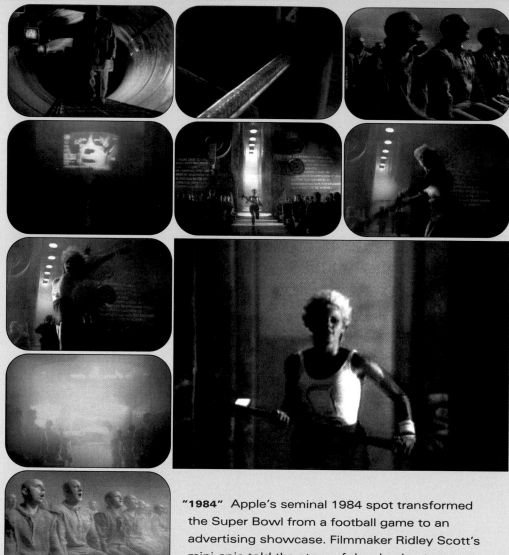

On January 24th,
Apple Computer will introduce
Macintosh.
And you'll see why 1984
won't be like "1984."

"1984" Apple's seminal 1984 spot transformed the Super Bowl from a football game to an advertising showcase. Filmmaker Ridley Scott's mini-epic told the story of devolved automatons shuffling in and watching Big Brother's harangue on an overhead screen. An athletic blonde, outrunning the "thought police," hurls a sledgehammer at the screen. The award-winning ad set the scene for the wildly successful introduction of Apple's Macintosh—without ever directly describing the product.

toward the screen wielding a sledgehammer, pursued by ominous "thought police" with face masks. Big Brother's harangue continues: "We are one people. With one resolve. Our enemies shall talk themselves to death. And we will bury them with their own confusion. We shall prevail!"

After winding up, the woman hurls the sledgehammer. The screen explodes in a blinding flash of light. "On January 24th, Apple Computer will introduce Macintosh. And you'll see why 1984 won't be like '1984,'" says the announcer.

Viewers may not have understood *all* that Apple intended to convey—that here was a user-friendly computer for the masses; that the woman represented youth rebelling against oppression; that she was smashing a symbol of Big Blue, IBM; and that Apple was a David to this Goliath. But they got the gestalt. This eerie spot, which never showed the product or even explained what it was, spoke to them.

Before Macintosh, Apple's future looked dicey. IBM had swept past it, Apple's two recent introductions had bombed, and its stock had tanked. Macintosh could change Apple's fortune and the way the world worked.

"Computing had been in the hands of a close-knit elite, and we were going to bust up that cabal and give the power to the people," says the ad's copywriter Steve Hayden (who has overseen the IBM account at Ogilvy & Mather and is now vice chairman there). "Macintosh was leading a revolution, taking power away from big business and big government and putting it in the hands of the people." Apple's mission was more ambitious than just convincing viewers to buy something they didn't know they needed—a twenty-pound machine that cost $2,495, real money in 1984. It aimed "to stop the world in its tracks…to let everybody know that something terribly important has just happened," he said.

In 1983, Apple cofounder Steve Jobs had clipped an article about how *Star Wars* was marketed to seem like a spontaneous hit when its success was actually meticulously orchestrated. Jobs wanted that lightning to strike again.

Chiat/Day wanted a commercial to play to the issues of the day: the antigovernment Reagan revolution, women's lib, and the rise of automation. During a meeting, Chiat/Day president Lee Clow doodled a storyboard showing a guy watching Big Brother on a TV, when a girl bursts in with a baseball bat and smashes the set.

Art director Brent Thomas later refined the vision, sketching the sinister monolith. British filmmaker Ridley Scott imbued the mini-epic with a German Expressionism sensibility and blockbuster production values. Scott hired 200 extras and had a seven-story set constructed on a soundstage at London's Shepperton Studios.

Initially, Apple planned to run "1984" on January 1 college football games. But the computer wouldn't launch until Apple's January 24 shareholders' meeting, so the airing was postponed. Jobs worried about whether computer buyers actually watched the game. Chiat/Day chief Jay Chiat worried that another advertiser, perhaps Sprint celebrating the January 1 breakup of AT&T, would preempt the *1984* theme. Apple's directors worried about the spot's dismal effectiveness score in consumer testing. When the board first saw it, the room went silent with misgivings. One director suggested that the agency unload the ad time it had reserved. Chiat/Day sold 30 seconds each to United Air and McDonald's, then pretended it couldn't get rid of the rest. So the board grudgingly—and fretfully—approved its airing. (Legend has it that Apple's cofounder Steve Wozniak took out his checkbook and offered to split the cost with Jobs.)

As it turned out, their worries were for naught. Almost 100 million viewers —46 percent of American households—watched Apple's visually stunning tease. The Monday after, 200,000 consumers flocked to dealers to view the Mac, and 72,000 bought one in the first 100 days, exceeding Apple's goals by 50 percent.

The ad ushered in the era of advertising as news: The three major TV networks replayed the spot as a story on nightly news programs. "1984" went on to sweep awards shows and became *Advertising Age*'s 1980s Commercial of the Decade. It also marked the beginning of the new era of integrated marketing communications.

In the next year's game, Apple tried for another touchdown, but fumbled. The company's new 60-second, $600,000 commercial, "Lemmings," was designed to pique viewers' interest in Apple's new business systems. In a desolate and macabre landscape, a line of blindfolded, conformist executives whistling "Hi Ho, it's off to work we go," shuffled along, one after another—right off a cliff. In the end, a freethinker removed his blindfold just before the precipice to choose an alternative.

Tony Scott, brother of Ridley Scott, directed the wasteland scene at the EMI Studio where much of the original *Star Wars* was shot. Apple worried that the spot would invite unwanted comparison with "1984," that it would denigrate the very managers who might buy it, or that it was too self-indulgent. The company reserved a one-minute time slot, canceled it, reinstated it, and

"LEMMINGS" In Apple's unfruitful "Lemmings" spot, a somber voice intoned, "On January 24, Apple will introduce the Macintosh Office. Look into it or go on with business as usual."

canceled it again. At the last minute Apple decided to go for broke, forked over $900,000, and sent off 85,000 cushions with its logo to pad the wooden seats at Stanford Stadium. Newspaper ads starkly warned viewers that if they "go to the bathroom during the fourth quarter, you'll be sorry."

Instead, it was Apple's management that was sorry. "Lemmings" tumbled, like the IBM minions it spoofed, because it alienated traditional business computer buyers and promised what the company couldn't deliver. The Macintosh Office, a line of business products built around the Mac, wasn't ready.

Nor was Apple ready for what followed. As sales slumped, Apple shuttered three of six factories, cut 20 percent of its employees, and in 1986 fired Chiat/Day and Jobs. And it steered clear of the Super Bowl until 1999.

The Super Bowl's commercial importance, unrivaled by any other single program on television, raised the stakes in adland and was a stage for phenomenal successes —and failures.

3

THE EIGHTIES

APPLE'S "LEMMINGS" wasn't the only standout on Super Bowl XIX in 1985, as 38 million viewers watched the San Francisco 49ers demolish the Miami Dolphins. The government actually stood down, postponing Ronald Reagan's presidential inauguration to January 21 in deference to Super Sunday.

Chevrolet, which had been the biggest sponsor of SB XVIII, balked at the $525,000 per 30-seconds price (up from $445,000 in 1984), but Ford, Nissan-Datsun, and Volkswagen rolled in. Inspired by Apple's success, IBM ran thirteen spots that day. The 49ers quarterback Joe Montana seemed to be in as many, touting Diet Pepsi, Ford Thunderbird, AT&T, Wilson sporting goods, and Schick razors. (Lady sheriff Jennifer Wallace, Montana's fianceé, arrests gunslinger Montana so he'll take her to the dance clean shaven.)

People weren't the only stars. Bright ideas also twinkled. In Sony's enigmatic charmer, the ultimate couch potato moves from birth to death on a sofa before fading out, leaving just a pair of slippers behind.

Once the king of the supermarket, by 1985 cans had lost their cachet: they're clunky, heavy, leave rusty rings, and are unsqueezeable. The National Food Processors Association, the Can Manufacturers Association, and the American Iron

"LIFETIME" Sony pitches its Trinitron television as a set that can grow old with you— and then some.

and Steel Institute joined to promote the beleaguered container as healthful and nutrient-preserving, using a high-tech Super Bowl commercial.

The mission was to explain why the metal can is part of the space age and dispel misconceptions about the nutritional value of its contents, said Millie Olsen, creative director of the spot. "To counter this irrational prejudice, we went associative rather than super-rational."

They spent $155,000 to animate a robotic femme fatale, the first character with truly fluid, human movement created by a computer. While the android swiveled in her spaceship kitchen, opening floating cans of vegetables and lighting a candle at a touch of her metallic fingertips, the sultry voice of Kathleen Turner announced, "Even in the year 3000, the question will be, 'What's for dinner?' The answer will be in a package that saves energy, nutrients, and trouble—a package that can last the three-year journey to Jupiter and back. Even in the year 3000, we see the brilliance of cans." Alas, a decade later, canned food still ranked far below fresh and frozen in people's minds.

Equally startling was Stroh Brewing Co.'s wunderhound. In Stroh's first forty-six-word, two-bark commercial, four men are playing poker when one sends his golden retriever to fetch a cold one from the kitchen. The dog obliges. The camera stays behind with the men, who sit transfixed by the sounds of the refrigerator opening, bottles being uncapped, beer pouring, and then…lapping. Alex's owner shouts, "Alex, you better be drinking your water!"

Alex doesn't really do anything—except charm viewers who imagine him opening the fridge and manipulating the bottle opener. The pooch got attention, but Stroh's ultimately feared its beer would be too closely associated with dogs. They crated him, then relented two years later to promote Stroh's Light and Stroh's regular brew. In one spot, a poker game is interrupted by the delivery of a side of beef and a case of Stroh's. No one's sure who ordered the goods until it's clear a female poodle is part of the order.

In another commercial, molten steel is forged into a sword, molded by a laser beam, and brought to salute by "one of a few good men with the mettle to be a Marine." Even by military standards, $1 million for airtime is real money. Yet the Corps joined the elite cadre of those paying that, because the now all-volunteer armed forces needed recruits. Potential Marines tend to be football fans, and 80 million of them were watching.

"BRILLIANCE"   A sexy, scarlet-eyed, metal-skinned woman from the year 3000 talks about the "brilliance of food in cans" from her Jupiter-bound space home, in a pitch for the Canned Food Information Council.

BY XX, MARKETERS regarded the Super Bowl as ad Mecca, the place where advertising should be super-exciting, super-dramatic, super-provocative, super-attention-getting, and super-creative. (And one marketer was to find in 1986 that failing here was super-disastrous.)

NBC had sold all fifty spots by Halloween. Veterans like Anheuser-Busch, the National Dairy Promotion & Research Board ("Cheese, Glorious Cheese"), and Northwestern Mutual climbed aboard. IBM alone represented the computer field with a dozen spots. Super Bowl newbies nabbed more than half of the available minutes.

Timex went to great depths (fifty feet below the Red Sea) to trumpet the durability of its new Atlantis 100 quartz sports watch. For twenty-two years, respected reporter John Cameron Swayze had narrated all manner of torture tests for the watch, from a high dive off Acapulco's Perla Cliffs to a washing

"ALEX," "ALEX II"   Is Stroh's beer-fetching dog (left, center) putting his muzzle in the merchandise? In a return engagement two years later (right), Alex the party hound sends out for beer, beef, and a canine consort.

"THE SWORD" The Marines hoped to recruit a few good men.

machine's spin cycle to a trip through Rover's digestive tract. If this watch could take this licking and keep on ticking, surely it could survive whatever rigors *your* wrist dished out. When Swayze retired in the mid-1970s, how well watches told time seemed less important than how they looked. Timex then tried different approaches to make its products into status symbols.

For a $1-million-plus epic, Timex sunk an eighty-foot, 1.5-ton replica of its new watch on the ocean floor. As eerie, synthesized music punctuated by unnatural screams and whale voices sound, deep-sea divers gracefully, almost balletically, vacuum the silt from this Atlantis, on whose face is—impressively—the actual current time and date.

The largest advertiser in XX, Sears Roebuck & Co., plunged for six spots alerting the world to the advantages of its new Discover Card: Consumers earned "real dollar dividends" every time they used it. Automotive accessorizer Durakon Industries also went to great depths, pouring almost $1 million— its entire ad budget—into graphically illustrating the benefits of its Duraline rubberized liners when a ton of bricks hits a truckbed. Years later, Durakon claimed, people remember that ad.

Alas, they also remember Burger King's "Nerd," featuring Herb, the only man in America who'd never tasted its signature hamburger. In 1986 Herb's parents, teacher, and chums all try—and fail—to get the balding, bespectacled dork to come to his senses and try a Whopper. Rather than lure new stomachs or succeed Wendy's Clara "Where's-the-Beef?" Peller as the next American fast-food folk hero, the half-baked Herb hurt Burger King instead. Critics panned Herb as "over-hyped and under-interesting" and the "most elaborate advertising flop of the decade."

Still, more commercials connected than misfired. Sprint crowed about its fiber optics network, "Clear Across America." Dow Chemical Co. introduced Touch Tech Lab, and Chrysler its sporty Daytona Turbo. Oppenheimer Funds cast animals as metaphors of bewildered investors: An ostrich buries its head in the sand, a dog chases its tail. RC Cola tweaked Coke and Pepsi: A tyke redeems their discarded cans to buy RC.

"ATLANTIS" With just a spoken postscript—"The Atlantis 100, because two-thirds of the earth is covered with water"—this Timex blockbuster conveyed mystery, danger, and urgency.

And in a James Bond spoof, Ninja warrior–assassins' shots miss actor Pierce Brosnan and punch two holes in a Diet Coke can from which refreshment gushes into two glasses for him and a gorgeous gal-prop.

But there was mounting unease about the mounting tariff. IBM had gone from its dozen spots in XX to run in surrounding segments only. Northwestern Mutual, which had run in six of the past seven games, sat this one out because of the fee. Others bought 15-second segments, the first time this short ad-form ran here. And advertisers pressured CBS for free or discounted bonus spots in other programs.

SOON AFTER RALSTON PURINA bought Eveready Battery Co. in 1986, it imported outrageous bad-boy Jacko, who had boosted Energizer's share in Australia, to jolt its U.S. sales.

To promote Energizer's new, longer-lasting alkaline battery, the spiky-haired hunk jumped out of the TV, ran around smashing things, and then hurdled back into the set. In Super Bowl XXII (1988), he overpowered a surrealistic subway car to sear battery-endurance claims into viewers' memories.

Instead, Jacko seared Eveready. Americans spurned the maniac who power-slammed through doors, forcing Energizer to reverse course. Ten months later, it unveiled an irresistible pink spokes-hare who banged a drum through dreadful commercials for invented products. Although the Energizer bunny, a metaphor for perseverance and long life, never actually appeared on any Super Bowl, he is Energizer's most remembered ad symbol.

In 1988, advertisers shelled out a record $625,000 for 30 seconds. ABC plugged its upcoming Winter Olympics telecast. IBM enlisted Jamie Farr and Wayne Rogers. McDonald's unveiled its new Cheddar Melt sandwich. And the

"AD AGENCY," "BALLOON PAYMENT" Loquacious, straight-faced "Frank Bartles" was, in real life, Oregon hog farmer David Rufkaur; stone-faced "Ed Jaymes" was Dick Maug, a California contractor.

dog Spuds MacKenzie took to the ski slopes for Bud. An astronaut returning after her twenty-eight-year mission to Saturn got rich with New York Life, the insurance company, and E. & J. Gallo introduced the world to two down-home hayseeds, and to what was to become the hottest entrant in the coolest new spirits business, Bartles & Jaymes Premium Wine cooler.

The odd couple—one chubby and chatty, the other skinny and silent—starred in a wry series that took them to Super Bowl XXII.

In one spot, Frank says that buying Bartles & Jaymes would be a "personal favor to Ed because he took that second on his house and soon he's got a big balloon payment coming up." In another spot, Frank reports on Ed's "scientific program to determine which foods go well with Bartles & Jaymes coolers." Only kohlrabi and candy corn don't.

A masterful blend of sentiment and spoof, with characters of a kind rarely seen in commercials, these soft-sell spots assumed that viewers were sophisticated enough to get subtle jokes and tongue-in-cheek humility. Gallo's name was nowhere in the ads or packaging, an omission as deliberate as the duo's aw-shucks style.

By 1985, coolers, with sales over $700 million, were the fastest-growing beverage in the nation. But by 1992, after more than 100 copycat coolers had surfaced on store shelves, sales declined and the characters disappeared. They'd done 230 commercials.

It was the decade
that saw the Persian
Gulf War, a growing
focus on the use of
celebrities, and the
initiation of the Super
Bowl as a launching
pad for new products.

4

THE NINETIES

IN APRIL 1990, Bruce Cleverly cut short an ad campaign his team had spent two years developing. The commercials weren't criticized or ridiculed; they didn't mislead or offend. Rather, Gillette's marketing chief yanked spots for its new Sensor because they created too great a demand. Gillette simply couldn't make the razors and blades fast enough.

Gillette isn't the first marketer to use the game to launch a new product. But it's among the most successful. In a do-or-die effort to wrest the shaving market back from rivals' disposables, Gillette bet the house. It spent a decade and $200 million to develop the pivoting, face-hugging Sensor system and expected to sell 18 million razors and 200 million blades in 1990, following its four-spot (at $2.9 million) Super Bowl splash.

Instead, it sold 27 million razors and 350 million blades in 1990, corralling significant share of the European and American blade market and becoming profitable two years ahead of schedule.

For years, Gillette urged men to look and feel sharp in its advertising on sports programs. That message still resonated with older guys, but younger ones equated Gillette with "hollow, plastic, and blue." They'd embraced cheap throw-away razors (including Gillette's), but that only eroded Gillette's profits and brand name. Before

"THE BEST A MAN CAN GET"   Ads in 1989 primed the pump for Sensor's launch and instilled the idea that Gillette represents "the best a man can get."

THE SENSOR LAUNCH   Gillette ran its ads in nineteen countries and fourteen languages, and it budgeted an extraordinary $175 million for marketing in 1990. (Some went unspent when the ads created too much demand and were halted.)

its SB XXIV debut, Gillette hinted about Sensor in teasers on college bowls, promising to "change the way men shave forever." Those ads interspersed shots of active men with shots of the razor over a jingle. "I'm so many faces. It's plain to see. We give you all we have to give. For all a man can be."

In 1989, BBDO created five warm, slice-of-life music-video vignettes of handsome men running, swimming, rowing, and snuggling infants and women, then blended them into one Super Bowl spot with a computer animation demo of how Sensor's spring-loaded blades work. It repeated the formula in the next two Super Bowls, and Sensor sales multiplied.

In XXVII, Gillette bought two minutes. Using the same packaging, vignettes, and music as it did for Sensor, it hoped to duplicate that success with its new grooming Series. Alas, the Series got traction but never vaulted like Sensor.

THE PERSIAN GULF WAR began shortly before January 27, 1991, the 24th anniversary of the Super Bowl. Americans feared prolonged fighting or a chemical or nuclear attack; advertisers worried they'd appear out of synch or opportunistic. ABC, netting $800,000 for 30 seconds (twice the cost of an average prime-time spot), pumped up the patriotism quotient and provided a half-time update on the war.

On the marketing front there were other wars. "Diet cola" combatants Coke and Pepsi both changed plans at the eleventh hour. Diet Coke scrapped funny spots featuring actor Leslie Nielsen as a bumbling police detective promoting a sweepstakes. It kept "Crack the Code," its biggest Super Bowl promotion ever, but instead of Nielsen, it scrolled a message on the screen as a somber male voice urged viewers "to recognize what is truly important: our men and women serving in the Persian Gulf." Coke also announced its donation of $1 million to the U.S.O.

Coke's advertising—purporting that it was not advertising—struck some as phony and patronizing. *Ad Age* chided: "Coke made the wrong move, baby."

But Diet Pepsi, it seemed, made the right one, launching its "You got the right one, baby" campaign with a tuxedo-clad Ray Charles and the "Uh-Huh Girls" (Meilani Paul, Darlene Dillinger, and Gretchen Palmer) in slinky outfits singing backup. In one spot, Charles isn't sure "Uh-huh" has caught on, but an African tribe, worshipping Buddhists, and geishas belt it out to reassure him. In another commercial, Jerry Lewis, Charo, Vic Damone, Tiny Tim, a dog, and Bo Jackson audition to sing the jingle.

Pepsi canceled a promotion inviting viewers to call a toll-free number and sing the jingle to qualify for a prize: The government feared it would tie up the nation's phone lines and disrupt communications at a critical time.

Although Audi was the only auto advertiser in the game, it too was locked in a fierce battle—against its own image. After *60 Minutes* reported in 1986 that some Audis accelerated on their own, sales plummeted. In its first ad since its exoneration, Audi used grainy, fast cuts of its Quattro speeding through wintry weather.

7 UP made an issue out of being "Un." In one spot, a glass of cola undergoes an oil change, its brown liquid replaced by clear 7 UP. And Royal Caribbean sailed into the Super Bowl with three spots to take on land-based luxury resorts. While a montage showed

But with our service men and women in the Persian Gulf, we feel it would be inappropriate to run our lighthearted commercials at this time.

Thank you for your patience and understanding. And congratulations winners, from

The Coca-Cola Company

"CRACK THE CODE"
During 1991's Desert Storm, Coke got patriotic.

"PERFORMANCE" Ray Charles and the Uh-Huh Girls in their short, slinky dresses made Pepsi "the right one, baby."

vibrant vacationers, a narrator explained that Royal Caribbean was the one great resort in the world that "takes you to the great places of the world."

During Super Bowl XXVI (1992) while the Washington Redskins thumped the Buffalo Bills, the recession battered CBS. Although forty-two advertisers paid almost $850,000 per 30 seconds, spots sold so slowly that CBS had to cut deals. Lured in at the eleventh hour, General Motors bought one 90-second and two 30-second spots to tell Americans it heard their demands for quality. It was joined by Isuzu's Rodeo SUV and by Toyota celebrating its Kentucky workers who build the Camry.

There was little commercial glitz. "Only a few people dressed up for the prom; the rest came in their casual clothes," said Nina DiSesa, then executive vice president at J. Walter Thompson. Kellogg's urged folks to try its Corn Flakes, Sudafed showed how to fight a cold. Merrill Lynch pitched the Olympics two weeks later.

Before XXVI, Nike teased without exaggeration that it had paired Michael Jordan with "one of the most powerful icons of the twentieth century"—Bugs Bunny. (In 1991, Nike had used the duo in a 90-second marathon, adding animated character Marvin Martian.)

In a 60-second spot, four bullies disturb wascally wabbit Bugs Bunny's subterranean slumber and violently hurl him across a basketball court. Bugs straps on some Nikes, chortles, "What's up, jock?" and declares war on the thugs with Hare Jordan at his side in a game of hoops. ("Who'd ja expect, Elmer Fudd?" Jordan asks.)

"Audi quattro"

Frito-Lay scored by not showing up, countering the game by sponsoring the "Doritos Zap Time," a special half-hour episode of Fox's *In Living Color* that began as halftime began, when usually half the audience bails. Frito-Lay got eight spots plus a sweepstakes contest built into the programming. Vice president Steve Liguori wasn't sure if the Super Bowl was "passé," but thought it was time to start an end run. Fox quadrupled its audience in that half-hour, as viewers deserted CBS. Subsequently, the NFL beefed up the halftime show big time.

IN THE HEALTH WORLD, women call the shots. Yet pharmaceutical companies shook their test tubes on the Super Bowl. Why? Because some drugs are gender-neutral, some last minute deals were too good to pass up, and women were now watching in droves.

"TAKE CONTROL" With its new tagline, "Take Control," Audi aimed to own the idea of handling and control—"much as BMW owned performance and Volvo owned safety," said managing director Ben Hilverda. Spots showed power transferred automatically "to the wheels that can use it best."

"SEVEN SEAS" Royal Caribbean promoted itself as a portable resort.

That was the case in 1992 when Marion Merrell Dow pioneered advertising a prescription drug, Nicoderm, here. After directing ads at smokers, MMD wanted to talk to their families and physicians, too. So it presented the Nicoderm patch as more comforting than cold turkey and willpower for nervous, nicotine-starved airline passengers. Unaesthetic, maybe. Effective, for sure. Nicoderm became the leading nicotine-replacement product by far. Its factory could not keep up with demand.

Bristol Myers Squibb Co. also got hooked by a last-minute bargain. No doctor's recommendation, convoluted names of ingredients, or animatronic anvils pounding inside vibrating heads. Instead, in XXVI, Nuprin found its messenger in tennis star Jimmy Connors. The aging backache-sufferer had just defaulted to young Michael Chang in the French Open. "He seemed like a guy who fights and fights just to stay alive out there," said Hal Friedman, JWT senior vice president.

A year before, Texas Rangers pitcher Nolan Ryan tossed a baseball and testified for Advil. In one spot he confides, "Every season is more of a physical challenge. But after twenty-six years in the majors, I've learned to take care of myself."

In SB XXX (1996), Reggie White led a trio of NFL defensive stars on a nightmarish visit to Heisman Trophy winner Eddie George, to recommend he try over-the-counter Tylenol for pain. Johnson & Johnson ran another OTC play in the game: It and partner Merck boldly claimed that their Pepcid A.C. was the only one "proven it can prevent heartburn and acid indigestion."

Technically, Breathe Right strips had been conceived in 1987 by allergy sufferer Bruce Johnson, who used to shove a twist-tie from a bread package up his nose to breathe easier. Ultimately, he concocted a more professional nasal dilator—and licensed it to CNS Inc.

But really, Breathe Right nasal strips were birthed by the NFL. CNS sent

"HARE JORDAN"   Warner Brothers based its hit movie *Space Jam* on Nike's spot where Michael Jordan and Bugs Bunny repel thugs.

sample strips to each team. Eagles' running back Herschel Walker wore one in a 1994 game, and it caught on. CNS fanned the fever by sending a photo of Walker wearing it to other teams. Deion Sanders, Ricky Watters, William Floyd, and Jerry Rice of the 49ers wore them during Super Bowl 1995, branding it trendy. CNS parlayed the fact that eight of the ten touchdowns in SB XXIX were scored by players wearing its strips into its own touchdown.

During Super Bowl 1996, CNS distributed samples to all attendees and aired two commercials. "Love Me?" opens in the dark. A woman asks her fellow to "wear one." The sound of a package being opened follows. Lights go on; we see it's not a condom but a nasal strip so they both can sleep. "Annoyance Meter" humorously registered snores of those without Breathe Right. After the game, three out of every four adults knew the name, versus one in four a year earlier.

Yet in late 1996, studies suggested that Breathe Right strips weren't a cure-all. Sales tumbled even as CNS created team-colored strips in 2001 (purple and yellow for the Ravens and blue and red for the Giants) to honor the game that put it on the map.

With no Winter Olympics to lure away ad dollars, and no recession or war to dampen enthusiasm, marketers plowed ahead in SB XXVII (1993). Some of the fifty-six spots should have stayed in the barn.

"CONNORS/CHANG"
Tennis star Jimmy Connors aced for Nuprin. Initially, JWT fretted that the "Nupe It" theme was too blistering, too close to "nuclear." Research reassured them that it worked when athletes were added.

"THE CATCHER" After taking Advil, Nolan Ryan is ready for another nine innings.

While the Cowboys routed the Bills, Coopers & Lybrand made its TV debut. "The Super Bowl transcends a football game. Press attention, bragging rights, the opportunity to entertain clients, the reach," explained Brian Carty, national marketing director. "Who can put a price on it?"

NBC did: $28,333 a second, or $850,000 for thirty of them. Coopers & Lybrand's two spots cost each of the firm's 1,300 partners on average $6,000. For that they aimed "to shatter the stereotypes that accountants are boring and predictable." A funereal voice begins, "Competition is fierce. Financial pressures are unrelenting." We think the careworn executive is getting axed; turns out, he's presiding triumphantly over his annual meeting, presumably because he hired C&L.

Coopers & Lybrand called the price peanuts in the greater scheme of things. Critics called it a massive waste, as fewer than 100,000 viewers were in a position to hire the firm. It would have been cheaper to send each prospect a handsome bronze bust of himself, one analyst groused.

MILLER HAD OWNED BEER RIGHTS to the Super Bowl logo but had been MIA here for seven years. Its two spots in SB XXVII failed to staunch its bleeding. One featured former baseball catcher Bob Uecker tending bar at a crowded dive in the middle of nowhere.
His secret: "Location."

On SB 1992 and 1993, a squawky, animated red dot named Spot, with shades and high-tops, had edged aside the mellifluous-toned Trinidadian actor Geoffrey Holder extolling the "mah-velous" virtues of clear, caffeine-free 7 UP, to try to convince younger people to try it "every once in a while" as a break from cola. America turned a deaf ear and Un and Spot died young. They never said

"GET THE GOODS" Bob Uecker conspiratorially whispers the secret for Miller Brewing Co.

"INHALE" In a spot many Americans could relate to, Lee's luckless lad breathes in so deeply to squeeze into his jeans that he sucks a bird from its cage.

what 7 UP is all about—just what it wasn't. Subaru of America irked viewers even more than a pregame spot where Old Spice deodorant boasted that it "puts more power in your pits." Teasers showed parts of the subcompact Impreza as lines squiggled about the screen.

However, viewers warmed to Lee Apparel's humorous tales about embarrassing consequences people face trying to squish into too-tight jeans. Lee, squashed by the designer crowd in the 1980s, refocused to appeal to full-body types with charming, empathetic updates on the battle of the bulge. In "Silhouettes," a man watches through a shade-covered window as his lady-love struggles into her jeans, collapsing onto a dressmaker's dummy which, from his vantage, looks alarmingly like another suitor. In "Shower," a sprightly fellow emerges from the bathroom singing an aria basso, squeezes into jeans, and becomes a soprano. "Need a little more room in your jeans? Try Lee, the brand that fits," says a sympathetic narrator.

MARKETERS OFTEN USE CELEBRITIES to symbolize a relevant strategic idea or act as a security blanket—a familiar, alluring face that can break through a crowd of clones. Using a star is risky, of course, not just because a marketer gets tarred by his misbehaving hijinks, but because sometimes stars can draw more attention to themselves than to what they're pitching. Yet while only 16 percent of viewers typically remember the product in an aver-

"THE ABBEYS" The Alamo Rent A Car family, Doug and Nancy Abbey, paused on their multi-million-mile trip only to eat, sleep, and have a son, Robert, and a daughter, Catherine.

age commercial, adding a star can double that, Starch Research has found. Imagine what it could do on the Super Bowl. The record 134.8 million viewers who tuned in for XXVIII (1994) didn't have to imagine. They saw a screen full of them. Forty-three of the fifty-six spots (at $900,000 for 30 seconds) featured stars—so many that some sniffed there was "all hat and no cattle."

There *were* spots without stars, of course. Alamo Rent A Car showed a fictitious Abbey family on a thirty-four-year journey (okay, 90 seconds) through all 4,137,000 miles of Alamo territory.

But high-wattage athletes like basketball players Charles Barkley, Larry Johnson, and Shaquille O'Neal shone for Pepsi and Reebok, as did retired hoopsters Larry Bird and Michael Jordan for McDonald's and Nike. Bo Jackson appeared to race down the stairs of a skyscraper—to catch a can of Lipton Original he'd accidentally knocked off the roof. (Years later when a gullible fan asked how he'd done that, Jackson told her he was younger and faster then.)

Former coaches Mike Ditka and Bum Phillips and sportscaster Marv Albert twinkled for Bud Bowl VI. Alec Baldwin, Kim Basinger, Michael Caine, and Wesley Snipes pitched new movies. Christine Lahti was heard but not seen for Neon. Perhaps the company that has most consistently had its wagon pulled by star power is Pepsi-Cola. In 1994, in the celeb-heavy spot "Deprivation Tank," supermodel Cindy Crawford cooed that she'd "do anything for science." That turned out to mean going into isolation and going without any Pepsi. The unexpected results of that experiment can be seen at right.

"DEPRIVATION TANK" Nutty professor Michael Richards (Kramer on *Seinfeld*) put Cindy Crawford in a Pepsi deprivation tank—from which she emerged as Rodney Dangerfield.

PART TWO

THE
ARENAS

Game-day beer ads
poured it all on, using
everything from
hard-partying dogs
and animatronic frogs
to brand names
personified by jostling
bottles to woo
those watching.

5

THIS BOWL'S FOR YOU

FOR MORE THAN A DECADE, on the Monday after Super Bowl Sunday, the Anheuser-Busch team has huddled in its St. Louis war room to begin planning the lineup for next year's game. Deciding what to run is an industry unto itself. Typically hundreds of storyboards are hurled around under a poster-size photo of a rhesus monkey with Marlon Brando's face. (The actor had briefly considered rasping "Bud-weis-er," in a Super Bowl spot but ultimately decided against it.) Some 400 people at Anheuser-Busch's ad agencies and production companies work throughout the year on what will air during those precious moments.

Approximately twenty-five commercials are produced from dozens of concepts and screened before focus groups and Anheuser-Busch management. (One year August Busch IV, then VP of marketing, and Robert Lachky, VP of brand management, liked the idea of a turtle running for president of the United Swamps of America but decided it was, well, too political and potentially alienating.) Commercials can be nixed up to the last minute by unenthusiastic reactions, or doctored. "We're not asking people to be art directors, we're asking their opinion as someone who watches TV," Lachky says. "We don't wing it. We can't."

In addition to trotting out the majestic Clydesdales who've clip-clopped for Bud

"SEPARATED AT BIRTH" In 1999, focus groups almost consigned one Budweiser ad to the doghouse. Anheuser-Busch saved it by making clear that years had passed between when a Dalmatian pup picked for a fire-truck job gives a raspberry to a sibling passed over, and when the second dog is seen riding magisterially aboard the Clydesdale beer wagon.

since 1852, the sole beer advertiser in the 1986 game amused with its "Gimme a Light" spots in which tavern customers receive a flaming torch, burning baton, or flashing police car bubble instead of a light beer. In "Beer Trek," a body-less bartender begs a space traveler who asks for "a light" to be more specific. Finally he blasts the uncooperative patron into space with a forceful beam of photons. In Super Bowl XXI, a young Thomas Edison explained the complicated procedure of creating an electric light. "Well, it's very nice, Thomas. But I wanted a Bud Light," his friend replied, pouring the beer into the lamp's glass cover.

Another star of Anheuser-Busch's lineup was a white English bull terrier with a football-shaped head and a dark brown splotch around one eye— Spuds MacKenzie.

The Original Party Animal (who was actually a female) soon became a cult figure (adorning beach towels, key chains, and T-shirts) and by 1987 was a major player in Bud Light ads. As a "senior party consultant" in Hawaiian shirt and shades, or in a captain's outfit with silk ascot, Spuds always had his beer cooler and a bevy of female friends nearby. In Super Bowl 1988, Spuds careened off a 90-meter ski jump and lounged in a ski lodge promoting moderate consumption of alcohol.

Costuming and camera tricks made Spuds look the live wire, and Anheuser-Busch's publicity machine kept him high profile. He toured with a trio of Spandexed honeys, the Spudettes. There were reports he had died in a plane crash, been electrocuted in a hot tub, or drowned while strapped to a surfboard during filming, all orchestrated by A-B.

Spuds sent Bud Light sales soaring. But in 1989, sensitive to critics' protests that he appealed to those too young to drink—and concerned that he might

"SPUDS" Spuds MacKenzie was seen living the good life at a disco and, here, in a spa.

overpower the brand—Anheuser-Busch dispatched him to the doghouse. "He's such a dude, we had to be careful not to make a Spuds commercial with Bud Light, but a Bud Light commercial with Spuds," admitted Budweiser's Joe Corcoran.

"FROGS" Although creators of a Ranier Beer spot from the 1970s called Bud's frogs a rip-off, DMB&B's art director Michael Smith claimed they were inspired by his childhood pet bullfrog, named Bud. Ironically, DMB&B was fired soon after the frogs debuted, after more than seventy-five years with Anheuser-Busch.

WITH SIX SPOTS LAUNCHING the Bud Bowl in the 1989 game (costing $5 million), the world's largest spender at the world's largest single sporting event made football history (see "The Battle of the Bottles" on page 60).

It was in 1995's Bud Bowl that animatronic frogs uttered the now-famous three syllables. Anheuser-Busch management immediately recognized it had another hit. Over the years, its frogs perched on rocks in a swamp or on a roadside, sequentially croaking Bud-Weis-Er. They try to cop a taste from a passing Bud truck, or get their tongues frozen onto beer cans. In one spot, a bullfrog hops in amorous pursuit of the sultry-voiced female frog who utters the second syllable, "Weis." (The Center on Alcohol Advertising found kids likelier to recognize the frogs than Bugs Bunny or the Power Rangers.) And Budweiser scored with other anthropomorphic critters. A colony of ants tugged home a bottle of Bud and poured it into their anthill, which erupted with party music.

Meanwhile, Bud Light was striking advertising gold with its Mr. Insincerity "I love you, man" campaign, spawned by a real-life encounter that DDB creative David Merhar had with his own dad. "Johnny" feeds his dad, brother, and girlfriends bogus New Man sentimentality to finagle their Bud Lights.

"COPIER" The 1997 Bowl featured Louie, a Bud Bowl bottle, and a new "What Do We Have Here?" spot. A salesman tricks an office worker into buying a photocopier that churns out Bud Lights. Actually, the con man's partner inside the copier furnishes the illusion.

"LOBSTER" About to be cooked, a lobster takes a valuable hostage.

In Super Bowl XXX (1996), the Bud moocher sneaks into a posh Hollywood party and tries to flatter Charlton Heston into relinquishing his Light. "You are so special. That chariot thing you did and the water stuff," he says. Heston doesn't bite, but he does coach Johnny on how to deliver his "I love you, man" line. That year, while the beer market fell, Bud Light sales and market share rose: It had become the nation's second largest beer as well as its fastest growing.

By 1997, Johnny and the frogs were losing heat. So Anheuser-Busch went across the pond to recruit a reptilian family headed by wisecracking Louie, a curmudgeonly lizard so obsessed with landing the frogs' endorsement contract himself that he hires a ferret to do them in. This assassin theme percolated up when Anheuser-Busch asked its agencies for an idea to top the frogs. Goodby, Silverstein art director Todd Grant and copywriter Steve Dildarian snarled that they'd "like to kill those frogs" because it would be so tough to beat them, then realized they'd hit on an idea that just might.

In a gaggle of ads, Louie and his side-kick, the iguana Frank, grumble that the frogs got tapped even though "our audition was flawless." They plot the hit ("every frog has to croak") but bungle the execution. They drop an electrified bar sign into the swamp, but later commercials revealed that the char marks on lily pads where the frogs had perched didn't mean they'd been electrocuted.

In 1998, Budweiser paid more for eight *minutes* on SB XXXII ($16.8 million) than

"REX" Rex remembers his younger days when he chased Budweiser trucks.

"WHASSUP" After Anheuser-Busch ordered surgery to shorten the spots, "Whassup" became a byword.

the average candidate spent to win a seat in the U.S. Senate. In a new spot, a guy shopping with his girlfriend follows some power cords under a skirt rack and finds other guys hiding out with a TV and their Bud Lights. ("Psssst! buddy...over here...in Petites.")

By SB XXXIII, tired of criticism about the negative influence of the swamp croakers on children and antsy that its quarrelsome lizard would make Budweiser too downscale, A-B prepared Louie's swan songs. In one spot, the frogs give Louie a literal tongue-lashing. "Slap the punk," cries one. The effort must have done in the frogs, who faded away that year, replaced by a desperate lobster in a restaurant kitchen, being whisked to a

"SATIN SHEETS" In a 2002 spot, a man whose wife lures him to bed with lingerie and a bottle of Bud Light dives for the beer, slides on satin sheets, and sails right out the second-story window. A tree branch snags his underwear on the way down, leaving him boxerless to face his startled neighbors.

pot of boiling water. Frantic, he reaches out with his claw and snatches a bottle of Bud from a passing tray to hold off the chef. Kitchen workers try to get the crustacean to release its hostage. No deal. The creature backs his way out to freedom, a customer opts for the sirloin instead, and "lobster" is erased from the specials du jour.

In 2000, Anheuser-Busch had another critter up its corporate sleeve. Dog actor Rex can only cry on cue by drawing on his saddest memory—chasing the Budweiser truck, only to smash head-first into a lawn-service van.

And of course, there was "Whassup." The concept for the 2000 block-buster came from music-video director Charles Stone's two-minute film, *True.* DDB's team saw Stone and his Philadelphia buddies sit around and greet each other with "Whassup?!" and saw that it represented the same things Bud did—male camaraderie and friendship.

DDB hired Stone to direct and star in the appealingly hip adaptation. Three days into casting calls they scrapped the idea of actors in favor of using Stone and his comrades. Young guys liked the first "Whassup" spot in December 1999, but older ones and wholesalers blanched. Anheuser-Busch trimmed the ads and the "Whassup?!" vamping. Soon viewers were high-fiving the campaign and Bud for being cool.

"CEDRIC" Smooth, funny Cedric watches his amorous intentions foam away as his Bud Light explodes all over his dream date.

"MINIFRIDGE" In a fake TV show, a killer robot attacks a minifridge loaded with Bud. A huge hammer catapults from the fridge to destroy it.

Stone, watching TV at home with a bottle of Bud, answers the phone. His friend, "B," is doing the same at his house. "Dude, what's up?" B asks. "Nothin'. Watchin' the game, havin' a Bud. What's up with you?" B responds in virtually the same language. "True, true," they both add. Friends and roommates walk in and everyone utters "Whaasssuuup?!" It was soon heard everywhere—muttered by DJs, on websites, in spoofs, in the news. Anheuser-Busch even parodied it in such spots as "Wasabi," set at a Japanese restaurant. In SB 2001, back aboard his spaceship, an alien disguised as a dog is asked what he learned on Earth. He answers, "Whassuuuup?!"

Anheuser-Busch continued to set the stadium on fire in 2001 and 2002. In one misadventure, when a guy's arm gets caught in an elevator, strangers ignore him and help themselves to his six-pack.

Some say that A-B's $2 billion annual marketing budget would make anyone a player. But car companies and fast fooderies with deflated results from inflated ad budgets put that myth to rest. It's the manner in which Anheuser-Busch has used the Super Bowl to tap mainstream American humor, target "real guys" without undermining product quality, and run enough branding spots to appease retailers that makes these beermeisters admeisters, too.

THE BATTLE OF THE BOTTLES

Just before kickoff on XXIII (1989), Mars aired the first pet food commercial ever in this milieu of masculinity (introducing Kal Kan's new name: Whiskas). Toyota's feisty gray-haired ladies defied expectations by "punching it," zipping their Camry into the fast lane. Merlin Olsen arm-wrestled for FTD Florists. Nike had a hit with "Bo Knows." But the standout ad of SB XXIII was Bud Bowl I. Probably more people remember that simulated football game with helmeted long-necked bottles of Bud and Bud Light facing off in a computer-animated gridiron battle than recall that the 49ers beat the Bengals, 20–16.

"BUD BOWL" Several player-bottles wore TV cameras on their helmets. There was even a "live" cutaway to a bar in Cerveza, Texas, a Bud Bowl player's hometown.

Anheuser-Busch was a big Super Bowl player, but a licensing deal with the NFL barred it from even referring to the game in commercials. Miller had already paid mightily for that privilege. So A-B concocted its own game (and, ultimately, institution).

In the six-commercial debut spoof of the bowl, NBC sportscasters Bob Costas and Paul Maguire provided a play-by-play pun fest of the bottles passing, blocking, and tackling. "Let's kick some Bud," exhorted coach Ara Barleyseekin to wide receiver Brew Beerson. A media guide provided bios of such characters as coach Vinnie Lembrewski from Hopstra U, Ed O'Budovich from LoCal State, and "bone" vivant team owner Spuds MacKenzie.

The coaches were short, round bottles; the long-neck linemen wore protective collars. There was even the NFL's pompous use of Roman numerals. To keep the outcome secret, the sponsor taped different endings. Bud won Bud Bowl I, 27–24, with a last-second field goal.

None of this came cheap. Anheuser-Busch spent $5 million on the spots, created before computer animation by a tedious stop-action process. It took ten hours to shoot two seconds of film. A-B constructed a Ping-Pong-table–sized replica of Busch Stadium and stacked it with thousands of individual Bud cans to suggest a crowd. It was, to a typical beer commercial, as one analyst said, what *Who Framed Roger Rabbit* was to the old Looney Tunes.

From the start, Anheuser-Busch played the Bud Bowl as a retail promotion tied to a drawing that ultimately paid some lucky participant $1 million. But it was A-B that won big. Viewers lapped up the parody and bought 200 million extra Buds in January, an unprecedented 17 percent spike. The DMB&B agency used it as a soapbox. "If you like the way these guys played," their own ad brayed, "call their agent."

In 1990, Anheuser-Busch bought five in-game spots for Bud Bowl II and fanned the hype. Brent Musburger and ex-player Terry Bradshaw hosted the tomfoolery, with characters like quarterback Budway Joe (in sunglasses) and the Freezer (a/k/a "The Appliance of Defiance").

Anheuser-Busch's January 1990 sales ballooned 19 percent—making the Bud Bowl its most successful promotion ever. "This is no place for the faint of wallet," conceded senior brand manager Joe Corcoran. But he kidded, "Next year, we'll sell ad time on the Bud Bowl." Instead Anheuser-Busch bought ad time—spending a record $8 million for seven spots in SB XXV.

In 1992, A-B focused more attention off the field than on it, showing an accident-prone fan searching for his Bud Bowl sweepstakes ticket. Bud Light finally won, 24–17. January Bud sales in grocery stores climbed 46 percent.

Joe Namath and actor Corbin Bernsen joined the brew-haha as coaches in 1993. Eerily, each time a Bud Bowl ad aired in the first half, the score of the bottle battle duplicated the real game's. That year's Super Bowl ended 31–10, and the Bud Bowl score was 35–31. Bud won.

To keep the pageantry of bottles playing football fresh, Anheuser-Busch kept drafting new players. Bud Bowl VII featured wacky castaways Iggy, Biff, and Frank watching the first part of the bottle battle while marooned on a desert island. Then, Iggy gets drafted into the game. At almost eight times the size of the average player, he powers an eighty-yard touchdown to push Bud ahead 16–24. By then, folks had wearied of the grudge match, and in 1999 Anheuser-Busch moved it to the Web. There, Bud squeaked by, 13–10.

New cars are
the priciest products
most consumers see
advertised on a typical
Super Bowl broadcast,
and automakers spend
princely sums to
drive sales there.

6

ROLL 'EM

EARLY ON, IT WAS THE BIG THREE automakers who found the game, with its patriotic overtones and largely male audience, the ideal ad venue. In short order, so did the foreign carmakers. The Super Bowl became America's automobile showroom.

Ford signed on to the big game from the start and made frequent pit stops here. In 1982, its Ford Ranger pickup rained from the sky, and the next year's game implanted the "Have you driven a Ford lately?" slogan in the American subconscious. Two years later, Willie Nelson crooned "On the Road Again" to pitch trucks. To get Lexus and Acura buyers to consider the Mark VIII, Lincoln urged SB XXVII viewers to "Drive Everything Else First." In 1995, cables holding a Lincoln Continental aloft suddenly snap. The car that is "the perfect balance of luxury and technology" lands in perfect balance on a floor-mounted pinnacle.

But Ford's star may have shone brightest in Super Bowl 1997, when its curvy new F-150 hit town. Its F-Series pickups were America's best-selling vehicle for thirteen years, and the F-150 had been its most popular model. Now, though, new rounded or "feminine" styling threatened sales. A "Built Ford Tough" ad had to get buyers past that perception. It began literally, with a leap: The new F-150 sailed 134.5 feet

"TRUCK" Ford, worried that the new styling of its brawny best-selling truck would be perceived as too feminine, emphasized toughness.

over nineteen previous models to lead the F-Series family of trucks. (The jump was filmed in a desert with nothing underneath. The trucks were later added by computer.)

In one of seven spots on SB XXX, tough guy Jack Palance won't let anything—even the Grand Canyon—keep him from bringing in the herd. He hops out of the cab, lassoes a rock formation to the F-150's hitch, and with his trademark sneer, defies Mother Nature by pulling closed the yawning gap. "Better get to the Grand Canyon…before we do," Palance growls. The F-150 remained the best-selling truck in the universe.

HONDA HAS RELIED on a playful, humorous approach to showcase its cars since its Super Bowl debut in 1995. That year a villain, dropped from a helicopter onto the roof of a speeding Civic del Sol, was sent airborne when the couple inside release its removable hard top. A love-sick assembly-line robot falls for the Accord, not just a "car you need…but a car you want" (1998). But perhaps American Honda Co.'s best Super Bowl presentation was the maiden voyage of its Odyssey, when the company turned to the colorful animation style of recently deceased pop artist Keith Haring (1995). While minivans sold well, "boomers saw them as un-hip mommy-mobiles, an admission of a lifestyle change," said Larry Postaer, executive vice president at Rubin Postaer & Associates, Honda's agency. "This reassured them." In one spot, a bright blue figure grows up and hooks up with a bright yellow figure to make a brilliant red baby. "Just 'cuz you grew up, got a job, got married, and had a family doesn't mean you have to get one of those, uh, those, you know," says actor Jack Lemmon.

In 1997, Honda took the kitchen-table debates—where families argue about what features they want in a new car—a comic step further. A family meets in an imposing, dark-paneled law office, where each member's attorney negotiates for the interests of his client, including four-year-old twins, an older sibling, and a big dog.

SB XXI (1987) was notable for the Giants' rout, CBS's record tariff ($600,000 for a half-minute), and for what may have been the first network TV spot where an advertiser lied—and admitted it. Toyota and Nissan were already established here when Isuzu asked the Della Femina ad agency for a local dealership spot in 1986. Rather than tack on details like mileage and price to existing film, Della Femina enlisted a lying sleazeball to make exaggerated claims, which superimposed captions rebutted. Audiences literally read between the lines.

Desperate to get the cars' selling points heard, they swallowed misgivings that "Liar" cut too close to the truth of their business. Jon Lovitz was their first choice for the reptilian announcer, but he wanted too much money. So they selected struggling actor David Leisure, who oozed like a punctured tube of toothpaste as Joe Isuzu. Among the wild claims made through 1989: "The amazing Isuzu I-Mark gets 94 miles

"FAMILY NEGOTIATIONS" Honda turned a family's haggling into hilarity, as lawyers argue for each member. At the end, Richard Dreyfuss's voice promises "something-for-everyone" in the Odyssey.

per gallon city, 112 highway," Joe deadpanned. (It's really 34 mpg city, 40 highway, the correction noted.) It sells for $9. ("Wrong. Prices start at $6,999.") The Trooper II has "enough cargo space to carry Texas." (The overlay clarifies: "79 cubic feet of it.") His I-Mark miraculously overtakes a bullet he'd fired from a .357 magnum.

When Leisure showed up at the shoot in a cast—he'd broken his ankle ice-skating—Della Femina placed him in a Formula One racing suit beside a theme park bumper-car ride. "I had a little problem here at Monte Carlo," he casually admits. The super explained: "He slipped in the bathtub." Most spots ended with his shark smile, "You have my word on it."

Joe Isuzu made Isuzu's name memorable, and "You have my word on it" became part of the vernacular. But news reports declared the cheeky ads ineffective, and dealers soon demanded more product-specific, image-lifting ads.

"MOM" The world just knew Joe Isuzu's mom was toast in SB XXI when the famous liar invited lightning to strike her if the 4x4 Isuzu Trooper couldn't "hold every book in the Library of Congress."

EVEN BEFORE THERE WAS a Super Bowl, Chrysler Corp. sponsored the old AFL. It's been a Super Bowl stanchion—with early-day "white hat specials" and later appearances by Chairman Lee Iacocca. "If you can find a better car, buy it," he exhorted. He solicited a $1.5 billion congressional loan guarantee, accused Americans of an inferiority complex about Japanese imports, and in 1975 announced hefty rebates to whittle down a 120-day backlog of new cars. On the Super Bowl in 1981, Chrysler ran nine spots (more than any other advertiser) to announce it was coming back. But it really scored thirteen years later in SB XXVIII, when Neon alighted.

Marketed simultaneously through Dodge and Plymouth, Neon was developed "in a dare-to-be-different environment," said marketing vice president Arthur C. "Bud" Liebler. "So we pushed the envelope in marketing as well." An hour-long "Road Trip" TV show in December 1993 chronicled the cross-country trek of four Gen-Xers in a Neon (Greek for "new"). Then came teasers that mentioned the car and hinted at its attributes but never showed it.

The car that *Automobile Magazine* said "blew our doors off" was finally unveiled in four "simple" spots in SB 1994. These ads were in fact exquisitely orchestrated to get people to fall for this friendly, personable car that looks cute, costs little, and respects the environment a lot. (That's why the Neon was always shown in white.)

A week after the Super Bowl, Chrysler recalled the car, threatening to gridlock elaborate marketing plans. Instead of lying low, Chrysler pressed forward full throttle with seventy-five commercials in the Winter Olympics and a computer game based on *Star Wars*.

"HANGAR" In one spot, the imposing doors of a huge aircraft hangar slowly opened to reveal a white Neon, and a friendly "Hi" flashed on the screen.

"TOPIARY" A spot recalled *Edward Scissorhands:* Shears madly clipped a topiary Neon as the narrator pointed out environmentally correct attributes and declared, "No matter what color you choose, we do our darnedest to make it green."

"TOWN CAR" One follow-up spot juxtaposed Neon's features with those of a Lincoln Town Car and concluded, "The rich, it would appear, do not have it all."

"ASTROLOGER" Cadillac hoped its irreverent, daring ad would titillate. Instead, female General Motors executives, themselves part of the target audience, protested that it was the wrong image to attract professional women. Critics howled that it was sexist and that its wisecracking duck cheapened Caddy's prestige image.

"ASSEMBLY LINE" This commercial used the George Thorogood rock tune "Bad to the Bone" and an assertive slogan: "It's good to be the Cadillac."

"BREAK THROUGH" "The legendary bloodline is about to boil," says the voice of Gary Sinise. In the 30-second version, the tagline declares that Cadillac is "a legend reborn."

ONCE THE SYMBOL OF SUCCESS in America, Cadillac had become a dowdy symbol of wannabe-ism, pimp-mobility, or geriatric drivers. The Cimarron, Allante, and Seville STS did little to bring back buyers who'd flocked to Lexus, BMW, and Mercedes, and Cadillac's share of the luxury car market nose-dived from 22.2 percent to 14.8 percent between 1990 and 1996.

Then came the Catera and $2 million ads featuring Cindy Crawford and an animated red duck. The supermodel is a bored princess in a medieval castle, dressed like a dominatrix in a black leather micro-dress and knee-high go-go boots. To add excitement to her life, a red duck wizard gives her keys to "the car that zigs."

Two weeks after it debuted on SB XXXI (1997), the ad was ditched. After a year-long hiatus, Cadillac was back in SB XXXIII (1999). Its new luxury SUV Escalade, known on the street as "Slade," had become a cool icon for rappers. GM didn't want to devalue its cachet, but wanted also to attract boomers with bulging bankrolls.

Three years later, even as sales kept falling and its average customers' age kept rising, Cadillac returned to launch the CTS on XXXVI. In "Break Through," set to Led Zeppelin's classic "Rock and Roll," drivers of a 1959 Caddy convertible and new CTS exchange admiring glances before going their separate ways.

PORSCHE CARS SOLD WELL during the 1980s era of conspicuous consumption. In 1997, when Porsche launched a racy $40,000 two-seater, ads aimed to erase some of that "ostentatious and overbearing" image by focusing "more on what the car actually does versus arrogant posturing about how fast it can go," said Goodby, Silverstein's Jeff Goodby. A Super Bowl spot showed the Boxster being fitted together by human hands. "Makes you wonder who builds other sports cars," Patrick Stewart mused sardonically. The scene shifts to a clangorous factory where soulless robots assemble a rival car.

SINCE 1960 all of Nissan's U.S. ads—including a Roy Rogers testimonial, "We Are Driven," and "Datsun Saves"—reinforced the Datsun name. So when it changed its name to Nissan in 1982, consumers were mystified. They thought its Pulsar was a wristwatch and its Maxima, a checking account. "People didn't think Nissan stood for anything," said Thomas Mignanelli, then executive vice president of operations.

"DREAM" He's in a Nissan Z Twin Turbo, engine roaring, being chased by a menacing motorcyclist, race car, and Hawker Hunter fighter jet. None can catch him.

In 1987, Chiat/Day tried to help with unconventional, soft-sell "Built for the Human Race" spots that ran through Super Bowl 1988. Yuppie car designers sat around bantering about human engineering and "little cocoons" that fit consumers' driving habits, interspersed with scenes of drivers and their Nissans. They were widely maligned as unnatural and unbelievable; Nissans piled up unsold.

New models—and ads to tout them—emerged. "We understand that a car fulfills a number of human needs, and that transportation is only one of them," a voice says as owners gaze lovingly at their Sentras. A futuristic fantasy by movie director Ridley Scott for its 300ZX Twin Turbo sports car was so hot that it steamed some viewers. Amid surrealistic effects, a guy recalls his *Blade Runner*-esque dream.

More than a dozen groups representing insurers and pediatricians complained that the ad glamorized high-speed driving. Nissan dismissed that, claiming the ad was "clearly fanciful," and ran it in SB 1990.

Eager to jolt Nissan's fuzzy image into focus, in 1996 Nissan U.S.A. president Robert Thomas approved two far-fetched concepts. In "Toys," GI Joe pulls up to a dollhouse in his snazzy red 300ZX to steal Barbie away from a disappointed Ken-like doll.

"PIGEONS" This Nissan special-effects extravaganza with a score from Kenny Loggins never talked about the car or its features.

In one of the series of enigmatic "Mr. K" spots, a boy chases a baseball into an underground garage where a mystical, bemused Japanese man introduces him to the history of Nissan cars. (Traditionally, Japanese companies had avoided icons from their country so as not to alienate xenophobes.) And the new slogan—"Life Is a Journey. Enjoy the Ride"— was so soft-sell that it could have reminded viewers of Nissan's much derided "rocks and trees" Infiniti commercials that showed only a series of nature scenes—no cars. Yet the unusual campaign actually reinvigorated Nissan.

Nissan passed on the 1996 contest, but Super Bowl 1997 found it back to its daredevil games. Three menacing puppet pigeons in flight goggles, helmets, and parachutes cruise the sky for trouble. They "leave their mark" on a shiny new black Maxima. The pigeon wing leader, voiced by John Ratzenberger, orders: "He's all yours, Sky Rat. Make it messy."

SINCE VOLKSWAGEN INTRODUCED the Beetle in the United States in 1959, it has urged Americans to "Think Small." In 2001, the German automaker had a change of heart. It envisioned big…real big.

VW had waved off the traffic-jammed Super Bowl after stalling here launching the Jetta, Golf, and GTI models in 1989. But when the sour economy detoured other car companies in 2001, VW bought two minutes and became that game's exclusive auto advertiser. Three "Drivers Wanted" spots introduced three new models. All had surprise endings, yet all were wry, witty, and gently absurd—i.e., classic Volkswagen.

"TREE" In "Tree," two young men toss sticks, rocks, a ball, and a sneaker to shake something out of a tree. Finally a red Volkswagen GTI thuds to the ground. "Next time," one guy tells the embarrassed driver, "let the clutch out easier."

In the wordless "Big Day," reminiscent of the wedding scene in *The Graduate,* a guy driving a Jetta VR6 nervously checks his watch at a railroad crossing. Wedding bells peal. The Jetta man does get to the church on time… to cause nuptial havoc for his ex-girlfriend, the bride.

IN ADDITION TO CARS AND TRUCKS, tires also rolled onto this ad field. Buying tires has long been a guy thing. Goodyear has known that—and that Super Bowl was a way to reach those guys. In the early days, testimonials and musical productions kept it top-of-mind.

Its airship *Eagle* kept it atop the game, literally, providing aerial coverage and marketing exposure. Goodyear's first blimp (it has had more than 300) was built in 1912 for military reconnaissance. By 1925, its lighter-than-air craft were primarily promotional; from 1967 to 1996 one has floated above every Super Bowl game except three: Pontiac, Michigan, and Minneapolis (grounded by weather), and Tampa, in 2003 (fears of terrorism). (In the 1977 movie *Black Sunday,* terrorists commandeer the Goodyear blimp to attack a packed NFL stadium.) For the "last American-owned tire company" the $12 million it spends annually to maintain three blimps pales compared with the publicity generated.

Goodyear had the skies to itself until the 1980s, when Metropolitan Life, Gulf Oil, and Fuji crowded in above the end zone. In 1987, Pepsi cut a deal with CBS for its *Slice* blimp to be Super Bowl's "official" airship. In 1990, Sea World's airship *Shamu,* shaped like a killer whale, joined the airborne flotilla. Other blimps floated in, and in 1996, Anheuser-Busch pressured NBC for an aerial monopoly, relegating Goodyear to pre- and postgame ceremonies.

"SKIER" In SB XXVII (1993), Goodyear showed water-skiers pulled by a Mustang to illustrate how the wet-traction Aquatred tires prevent hydroplaning.

Tires are a "distress purchase." Typical ads show some variant of a family on a dark road suddenly facing a truck careening toward them. Reliable tires get them out of a jam. But stringent regulations govern what companies can say about tire quality, so Michelin implied superior protection by raising the stakes on what's being protected. In a SB XIX (1985) "Because so much is riding on your tires" spot, diaper-draped "Amy" plays on a tire as Mom asks Dad why his car has Michelins and hers doesn't. "But sweetheart, they cost more…I drive to work, out of town…all you use your car for is shopping, driving Amy around…." Pause, as the value of her cargo sinks in. "I'll get you a set tomorrow," he says.

By 1989 Michelin had jumped from fourth to second place in the U.S. market. But in 2002, it dropped the tot and tire, which didn't cut it with the prime target of truck owners and speed lovers. The cool and relevant Michelin Man was reinstated, identifiable with Michelin in ways babies are not.

From the seemingly
endless reinvention
of the athletic shoe
has flowed a torrent
of inspiration,
all aimed at putting
one manufacturer's
footwear in front
of another.

7

SNEAKER WARS: GOING TOE-TO-TOE

JUST AS THE SUPER BOWL was the battlefield for what people put in their bodies (the cola wars), it was also a combat zone for what they put *on* their bodies. Although Converse and L.A. Gear tried to elbow their way in, Nike and Reebok were the titans—the Coke and Pepsi—in this battle. Since its founding in 1972, Nike has been a master of marketing, synonymous with stylish, big-budget, celebrity-packed technical tours de force.

But in 1987, after a seven-year run as America's top-selling athletic shoe, Nike was eclipsed by Reebok. It fought back with "Revolution," a 90-second, documentary-style commercial. There were black-and-white close-ups of regular folks and Michael Jordan and John McEnroe at their best, slow-motion shots of their shoes lifting and landing—and there was the music.

Nike paid a price bigger than the $500,000 for rights to the original Beatles "Revolution" recording. Capitol Records sued for $15 million, charging that Nike wrongfully traded on the Beatles' goodwill. And boomers resented Nike's misappropriation of a sacred piece of 1960s culture. Stung, Nike dropped the ad and let it be.

In fact, it was "being" just fine. Sport shoe sales were booming. "It wasn't like there were more feet, just that Nike and Reebok were covering feet more hours of

"BO DIDDLEY BASEBALL" Nike pitchman Bo Jackson knows about baseball—and other sports— but couldn't match Bo Diddley at guitar playing.

the day," said John Horan, publisher of *Sporting Goods Management News.*

Selling athletic shoes increasingly involved tapping the marquee value of star jocks. L.A. Gear lined up Karl Malone and Kareem Abdul-Jabbar. Reebok recruited basketball's Dominique Wilkins and football's Boomer Esiason. In 1985, Nike had signed Michael Jordan, then a twenty-one-year-old college junior (and ardent Adidas fan) just joining the Chicago Bulls to his own line of Air Jordan shoes—and a five-year, $2.5 million contract.

Nike's diadem grew to include, among others, Scottie Pippen, David Robinson, Alonzo Mourning, Deion Sanders, Jerry Rice, Ken Griffey Jr., Frank Thomas, Andre Agassi, and John McEnroe. In "The Barkley of Seville," Charles Barkley appeared to sing an Italian opera, prance through a basketball cathedral, kill a referee who called him on a foul, and have his shoes seized as punishment.

In 1988, Nike's "Just Do It" mantra against lethargy became the cornerstone of several blockbuster commercials, including the "Bo Knows" series, which ended on the 1990 pregame show.

As Bo Diddley and his band riff, athletes sound off about Bo Jackson, then Kansas City Royals' outfielder and Los Angeles Raiders' running back. "Bo knows baseball," testifies Dodger Kurt Gibson. "Bo knows football," adds Ram Jim Everett. "Bo knows basketball," confirms Michael Jordan. John McEnroe looks dubious. "Bo knows tennis?" he puzzles. "Bo knows running," marathoner Mary Decker weighed in, and body builders acknowledge he

"THE CATAPULT" L.A. Gear attempted to blast Nike out of viewers' minds with Karl Malone touting the Catapult shoe.

knows weights. Bo has his limits, though: Wayne Gretzky denies his hockey prowess, and Bo's off-key hacking at the guitar proves he doesn't "know diddley!"

Nike had first used multiple images of Bo—furiously pedaling a bike searching for "that Tour de Force thing," in basketball gear, tennis togs, as a hockey, cricket, and soccer player, surfer, weightlifter, auto racer, golfer, caddy, and jockey. The Bos noticed each other and complimented each others' shoes: Sony Bono walked on—he thought it was a Bonos commercial.

"DAN AND DAVE" Reebok's ads featuring decathloners Dan O'Brien and Dave Johnson asked America, "Who is the world's greatest athlete?" and promised to answer that question in the upcoming Olympics in Barcelona.

Wrestling with ideas for a sequel at a local bar, Wieden & Kennedy copywriter Jim Riswold heard lots of patrons' sugges- tions—Beau Brummell...Bo Derek...Bo Schembechler—before Riswold jotted "you don't know Diddley" on a cocktail napkin.

Within months, Nike was selling 80 percent of all cross-training shoes. The commercials played better than Bo did, however. Within a year they were benched, after helping Nike displace Reebok as number one. Other ads for Air Jordans costarred their director, Spike Lee. What makes you so great? Lee pesters Jordan. The "vicious dunks? extra-long shorts? short socks?" Finally, Lee decides, "It's got to be the shoes." In another ad, Douglas Kirkpatrick, a professor of astronautics, explains that Jordan "overcomes the acceleration of gravity by the application of his muscle power in the vertical plane, thus pro- ducing a low-altitude earth orbit."

Meanwhile, Reebok, named for an African gazelle, aimed to divest its image as a women's aerobic shoe company. In Super Bowl XXV (1991), it pumped up its new $160 inflatable Pump footwear and tossed aside an Air Jordan shoe. Subsequently, Dennis Rodman, Boomer Esiason, golfer Greg Norman, tennis player Michael Chang, and decathlete Dave Johnson also jabbed at Air Jordans.

L.A. Gear also targeted Nike in Super Bowl XXV to promote its new Catapult shoes. Utah Jazz NBA star Karl Malone sneered: "Everything else is just hot air." CBS refused the ads as offensive. BBDO, which had just won L.A. Gear's business, agreed, and soon after resigned the account.

David Ropes, Reebok's vice president for worldwide advertising and a for-

"LEGENDS" Reebok's Shaquille O'Neal, trying to impress hoops legends Wilt Chamberlain, Bill Russell, Bill Walton, and Kareem Abdul-Jabbar, is given a dustpan to clean up the court after he tears the hoop off the backboard.

"SHOOT PASS SLAM" Reebok's other Shaquille O'Neal spot, titled after a rap number from his debut album, was shot by twin brothers Allen and Albert Hughes, who directed the feature film *Menace II Society*.

mer Army helicopter pilot in Vietnam, likes risks. In XXVI (1992) he bet big that either Dan O'Brien or Dave Johnson, both relatively unknown athletes, would win the Olympic Decathlon and that Americans would grow to care about them—and their shoes.

How would Dan and Dave, who'd trained in virtual seclusion, fare when millions were looking over their shoulders? What if people weren't interested? And what of sprains and hamstrings? But trailing Nike by six market share points in the $5.8 billion sneaker market fortified Reebok's willingness to gamble.

Dan and Dave were introduced by their first names and with snapshots of them growing up. Voice-overs told of their sporting accomplishments. As the campaign developed, people voted for one or the other: A pretty young woman identified as Dan's ex-girlfriend broke a tie—by voting for Dave. (His real-life ex-girlfriend tried out for the part, but it went to a model instead. Everyone else cast was authentic.)

Reebok had two post-victory spots ready to wrap up the campaign showing the celebratory winner snoozing with a "Life is short. Sleep in" tweak. They never ran.

"LIFE ON PLANET REEBOK" On Planet Reebok life has "no limits, no pain, no cupcakes, no wimps, no lawyers, no mercy, no beauty pageants, no slogans, no fat, no excuses, no winners, and no losers."

"JORDAN'S DREAM" Nike contemplated Michael Jordan's retirement.

In June, O'Brien flubbed the pole vault and failed to qualify for an Olympic berth. Reebok ran substitute commercials, then a spot where Johnson consoles O'Brien. It galvanized the public. Dan and Dave didn't do what Ropes had hoped, but they did raise Reebok's profile. "Every paper in America had the story, and most had 'Reebok' in the headline," he mused. That helped narrow the Nike-Reebok sales gap.

At the 1993 Super Bowl, Reebok bracketed its commercials around Nike's super-hip Hare Jordan ads (see Chapter 4). Reebok's artillery: Shaquille O'Neal, the 7-foot-1-inch NBA rookie sensation.

In one spot, Shaq tries to win the approval of legendary greats at the renowned Hall of Fame Centers Club. Shaq demonstrates he's ready, but when he tries to hand over the shattered backboard, Wilt Chamberlain disdainfully pushes a broom at him and instructs Shaq to clean up the mess.

While Nike tried to hold on to the end of an era with Jordan, Reebok laid claim to a new one with a music video featuring Shaq rapping "Shoot Pass Slam" from his debut album.

In May 1993, Jordan had hinted that he'd retire. "What if my name wasn't in lights?...What if there wasn't a crowd around every corner? Can you imagine it? I can," Jordan had said from a dark gym. In Super

"GRANDMAMA" Charlotte Hornet Larry Johnson plays Grandmama, in a matronly flowered dress, gray wig, pearl necklace, and Cons. "She" steps through a door in a tornado and finds herself welcomed to Three-Point Land by a tiny referee, a Munchkin in the original *Wizard of Oz*. She needs Converse's new $110 BackJams to get home.

"EMMITT SMITH—LIVE—SUPER BOWL" Reebok had a back-up commercial in case the cameras or on-premises editing machines jammed on MVP Emmitt Smith's Instapump ad.

Bowl XXVIII (1994), Nike reprised the concept. Grainy pseudo-documentaries explored whether or not he had faked his retirement.

Investigator Steve Martin quizzes people from Harold Miner and Marv Albert to Spike Lee about what really happened to Michael, who's sighted playing semi-pro in silly getups.

THE CONVERSE "BLACK CONS" All-Stars were *the* basketball shoe in the 1960s. To make them so again, Converse raced to Super Bowl 1994, its first time here, with a minidrama take-off of *The Wizard of Oz.*

In that same game (XXVIII), Reebok made an insta-splash with an insta-ad for its Instapump. In the first half, a crew frantically videotaped players wearing Instapumps, edited it on premises, then ran a tape to the NBC Sports truck fifty yards away. As the last spot in the game, it was supposed to arrive with at least five minutes to spare. It got there with 2:50 left.

"STATE OF THE GAME" With the fanatic spot featuring Dennis Hopper, Nike delivered discomfort and edginess.

"LIL PENNY MOVIE" Little Penny Puppet, the puppet version of Orlando Magic guard Anfernee "Penny" Hardaway voiced by comedian Chris Rock, hosts a celebrity-studded Super Bowl party for Nike.

WILSON FOOTBALLS have been used in every Super Bowl, but XXIX (1995) was the first time it advertised here. Wilson toyed with biblical history and a cast of thousands to proclaim "The Right Equipment Makes the Difference." The leather slingshot and stone David uses to slay Goliath bears the "W" imprint. Some considered it blasphemous and offensive; Wilson called it "straightforward product as hero advertising."

Reebok sat out the Super Bowl in 1995, having broken new Shaq Attaq ads earlier. Nike might have been better off had it done likewise. Instead it spent $3 million on a 90-second, one-time ad featuring Dennis Hopper as Stanley Craver, a deranged, obsessed football fanatic. Hopper had appeared in fourteen effective Nike spots since 1993. Now, wearing a decaying football official's uniform, he sneaks into locker rooms and sniffs dirty sneakers ("I have smelled the shoes!") and delivers a loopy, impassioned ballad to football interspersed with confessions about his milk allergy and the soybean juice substitute that his mom gave him.

Nike briefly veered from celebrities for an emotional nod to Pee Wee football but soon returned to mock its own past ads.

In 1995, ad director Chris Zimmerman hinted that after a decade Nike would soon leave the game that had become so costly and hyped, "overshadowing the value that we are getting." Nike made one more appearance in 1998. "Evolution of Skin" unveiled its F.I.T. apparel line, as comfortable as a second skin. Thereafter, Nike decided to focus on niche marketing rather than looking big and slick.

Reebok also passed on the game after this, although in 2002 it issued 2,000 pairs of special edition Super Bowl sneakers emblazoned with the logos of the Rams and Patriots.

"EVOLUTION OF SKIN" Nike ads featured striking black-and-white scenes of naked athletes who appear at the end in color, clad in Nike apparel. NBC insisted that nipples and genitalia be obscured.

Faced with the soaring media costs of being in the game, not all marketers went after their goals straight up the middle. Some did ingenious workarounds to surround it.

8

END RUNS

"THE DORITOS ZAPTIME *In Living Color* Super Halftime Party" in 1992 was a milestone in the history of hijacking. By not advertising in Super Bowl XXVI, Frito-Lay became the talk of it.

Its end run was designed to get attention for its new bite-sized Doritos and strike at the championship's most vulnerable point—its banal midgame salute to gridiron greats or dancing snowflakes, when usually half the audience channel surfs or bails. For what Frito-Lay would have spent for two spots in the game it got eight commercials and a sweepstakes contest built into the program itself. In newspapers nationwide Frito-Lay urged viewers to follow it to Fox during halftime where *In Living Color* was the top-rated show among young men and teens, prime targets for Doritos. More than 20 million viewers did, making Frito-Lay's diversion worth $10 million at Super Bowl rates.

Still, Frito-Lay wasn't entirely satisfied. During a skit, Damon Wayans and David Alan Grier, as flamboyant gays, ad-libbed incendiary comments about Richard Gere and Carl Lewis. In 1993 (XXVII), Frito-Lay retreated to safer ground and became the first national advertiser to sponsor a Super Bowl halftime. Its show included a Michael Jackson performance.

Two Januarys later, the then-formidable Arthur Andersen & Co. ribbed companies for advertising on the Super Bowl, while applauding its own fiscally prudent end run. "At Arthur Andersen we'd love to be on the big game. However, the people we want to get this message to will probably be there and would miss our commercial." (Stadium fans don't see the ads.) Andersen ran that spot more than 150 times "for half of what it would have the cost for one spot in the ego bowl," managing partner Adrian Smith crowed.

Entrepreneurial companies have long tried to circumvent the high price of ads here, buying time on local markets or pre- or postgame shows. (Purina Cat Chow's ad on NBC's *Homicide* following the game cost one-sixth the price of a game spot and attracted 40 percent of the audience.) Others avoided paying for a spot by distributing samples near the game or holding sweepstakes connected to it.

In 2001, Subjex.com thought it had a clever way around the hefty tariff. It thought wrong. Right after Subjex announced its "Sneak" contest, awarding attendees $1,000 a second for getting its URL on CBS cameras panning the crowd, NFL attorneys obtained a cease and desist order. To mollify the NFL, the company changed the contest name and warned contestants they could be kicked out or fined. But when the NFL vowed to sue Subjex.com for damages and evict its contest participants, Subjex canceled the contest. Later, it boasted that the flap generated more publicity than the contest ever would have.

Anheuser-Busch invented the Bud Bowl as a way around Miller's "official" status and using all manner of promotions virtually edged Miller aside (see Chapter 5). Coca-Cola tried to steal the game's voltage without paying for the juice in 1994 when it sponsored seven hours of Super Bowl–related sports shows, yet didn't run in the game. In 1996, Coke hosted an interactive fan theme park to trumpet being named the official soft drink of SB XXX but

"DRESCHER," "TRUMP," "SPIKE LEE" Famous Big Apple faces Fran Drescher, Donald Trump, and Spike Lee pitch the "Big New Yorker Pizza."

was a no-show for the game's commercials that year. Another year it filled a *Friends* special that ran right after the game with Diet Coke spots.

Many marketers "surround" the event. In the pizza wars, where weapons are not pepperoni and sausage as much as marketing maneuvers like delivery guarantees, twofers, and ad blitzes, Pizza Hut turned to the coveted final pregame slot before kickoff. Three spots featuring well-known New Yorkers Fran Drescher, Donald Trump, and Spike Lee introduced its new Big New Yorker Pizza in the 1999 pregame.

In 2002, Pizza Hut introduced P'Zone, a "pizza you eat like a sandwich," with comedian Tommy Davidson. It also distributed P'Zone in malls and stadiums. "Pizza is Pavlovian," says Randy Gier, chief marketing officer. "If you see it on TV, it makes you want to jump up and lick the screen."

E-tailer MVP.com aligned itself with Super Bowl star John Elway: During the game from the sideline, Elway plugged MVP during interviews. CNS Inc. stuck its nasal strips on players' noses. For the fifth time, in 2002 rival quarterbacks donned milk mustaches together for the National Fluid Milk Processors. That same year, with signs plastered on phone booths outside the New Orleans Superdome, Tide proclaimed: "Because there are more than XXXVI ways to ruin your clothes."

While the NFL detests these guerrilla tactics that "shave the treetops," there's little it can do about them, says Jim Steeg, senior vice president for special events.

EVEN AS SOME MARKETERS AMBUSHED the Super Bowl, others rode its coattails. Just hours after SB XXXVI, Tom Brady, of the victorious Patriots, made a touchdown pass to David Patten, then uttered familiar words: "I'm going to Disney World." It was a ritualistic installment of Disney's "What are you going to do next?" commercial and the fifteenth anniversary of a campaign that began when Giants quarterback Phil Simms, flush with victory, responded to an inquiry about his plans. The promotion was actually conceived in 1986 by Jane Eisner, wife of Disney chairman Michael Eisner, during a conversation with the pilots of the record-setting *Voyager* aircraft. "What's next?" she asked, after they'd flown nonstop around the world. One answered, "Well, I guess we'll go to Disneyland."

Through the years, Super Bowlers, Miss Americas, and stars from the World Series and NBA all announced the same plans. In 1994, figure skater Nancy Kerrigan made a widely publicized gaffe. Kerrigan skipped the clos-

"PRIZE PATROL" Four men in blazers laid out champagne and flowers and serenaded Publishers Clearing House winner Mary Houston with "When You Wish Upon a Star." Houston screamed, "Pinch me and let me know I'm not dreaming."

ing ceremonies of the Olympics to join the Disney World Parade, where an open microphone caught her complaining. "This is so corny. This is so dumb. I hate it."

Others who answered the question included Cowboy Emmitt Smith, 49ers duo Jerry Rice and Steve Young, Packers wide receiver Desmond Howard, Broncos John Elway and Terrell Davis, and Rams quarterback Kurt Warner. In 2001, Disney passed over MVP Raven Ray Lewis to ask quarterback Trent Dilfer, because Lewis had been linked to a double homicide the year before. (Charges were dropped in return for pleading guilty to a misdemeanor charge of obstruction of justice.) The Magic Kingdom passed on the MVP three other times: In XXIII (1989), it elected Montana over Rice; in XXX (1996), it tapped Emmitt Smith over Larry Brown; and in XXXII (1998), John Elway was poster boy instead of MVP Terrell Davis.

Moments after Disney's winner declares his intentions, another game-day winner is usually surprised on live TV by a knock on the door. On January 21, 1998, Dave Sayer, ad chief of Publishers Clearing House, showed up at the home of retired schoolteacher Mary Houston. He identified himself and his mission and presented her with a check for $10 million.

The first winner, Phoenix accountant Mary Ann Brandt, answered the door with a mouthful of chicken and couldn't speak. That's the kind of response PCH has counted on since 1995 whenever its "Prize Patrol" pulls up to a sweepstakes winner's house during the postgame show. In 2002, Marcella and Jack Longnecker of Minnesota won the 33rd annual gig. A live commercial aired from their home during the postgame show.

"ISLAND GIRLS," above. For the Las Vegas Convention and Visitors Authority, a mom shows off her new tattoo to her horrified teen daughter. In **"WEDDING,"** below, a woman outside a wedding chapel smooches with a Spanish-speaking hunk and regrets that she has to return to her convention.

THEN THERE WERE SOME YOU NEVER SAW ON THE SUPER BOWL

In 1998, Vivus Inc. commissioned a commercial for Muse, its treatment system for impotence, to run on Super Bowl XXXII. A low-key, straightforward, factual spot voiced by actor Ed Asner noted how Muse can help many of the 20 million men with this problem and urged viewers to see their doctors.

Although the ad passed legal muster, it did not pass NBC's ad standards department, which deemed it inappropriate for broadcast during the Super Bowl. Hoffman/Lewis agency president Bob Hoffman deemed NBC's rejection "pure hypocrisy, considering the suggestive, sometimes lewd stuff that runs on daytime programming" and even in the game itself. Rival CBS ran it.

Dozens, if not hundreds, of commercials are Super Bowl "ghosts." Some were never seen by viewers because the network barred them. Others were

"GOLDILOCKS" In a Three Bears takeoff, Kim Cattrall saunters into an empty locker room and drinks a Coke, Diet Coke, and—this one tastes just right—a Pepsi One. The team returns to find her in a hot tub. NFL lawyers claimed the team locker room and uniforms too closely resembled those of the Chicago Bears. The NFL had a sponsorship in place with Coca-Cola.

canned at the last minute by a nervous client or sandbagged by unavailable talent. (George Michael missed a Coke taping in 1991.)

In 2003, the Las Vegas Convention and Visitors Authority earmarked $58 million to boost flagging tourism. Spots showed visitors cutting loose for the night but never mentioned or showed gambling. Nevertheless, the NFL, which demonstrated it had no issue with liquor or mud-wrestling girls, vetoed it because of the gambling implication.

In 2001, the NFL forced Pepsi One to do a last-minute about-face on an ad featuring *Sex and the City* star Kim Cattrall.

In November 1991, when Magic Johnson announced he was HIV-positive, it was advertisers who got cold feet. Johnson was to have starred in "Gotta Have It" Pepsi spots, but "missed" the filming.

In 2001, People for the Ethical Treatment of Animals (PETA) had budgeted $2.5 million to show real cows singing "I'm a steer, and they're steering you wrong…Listen now, I'm a cow, and I don't have long. Our sweet backsides would like to stay together. We don't want to be your leather" via computer animation. CBS mooo-ved it out of SB XXXV on the grounds that it doesn't accept "advocacy ads." The next year Fox rejected a PETA ad showing a man fondling a melon to portray veganism as sexy.

Food marketers
served up hearty fare
and hoopla to get
stomachs growling
among those who
"dine in" at halftime
on chips and dip and
are likely to "dine out"
at a fast-food restaurant
sometime soon.

9

FOOD FIGHT

WOMEN BUY MOST OF THE FOOD. Men watch most of the football. Why then do food marketers advertise on the Super Bowl?

H. J. Heinz did it in 1998 (Super Bowl XXXII) to reassure investors as much as motivate eaters. While 97 percent of American refrigerators store ketchup, people were grabbing salsa instead. To redirect those hands, Heinz showed plump computer-animated tomatoes bouncing, rolling, and squeezing into each bottle. Then the pour …slow, rich, luscious…and the bite: A child rapturously sinks his teeth into a burger. Heinz's strategy was first to grow the category it had created 125 years earlier, then to promote its leadership.

In that same Bowl, Hormel Foods told the world it had jazzed up its vintage canned meat dish. It plunked down $2.5 million—a fifth of its annual marketing budget—for two "in or out of the bowl, it's outta control" spots during prime chili season.

On average, each American eats about fifty pounds of pork a year. But in 1987, chicken was gaining fast, and the National Pork Producers Council, representing 80,000 hog farmers, felt it needed to make folks think "pork" more. It began reha-bilitating pork's image with "The Other White Meat" ads, and in 1995 looked to the

"BIG SQUEEZE" "Mine's Gotta Have Heinz," the ad pitched— the ketchup with twenty-five juicy tomatoes squeezed into each bottle.

"ALL NEW" One Hormel spot had all the ballyhoo of a new-car launch; another used disjointed quick cuts of its chili in various recipes.

Super Bowl to spread the word. "Taste What's Next" spots in the 1995 and 1996 Super Bowls were pedestrian. Great chefs cooked pork recipes with flair while a voice enthused, "It's the life of the party…the word on the street." Then, in SB 1997, pigskin and pork paired again. Two straightforward pitches about how good—and good for you—pork is ran in the pregame. Then came the Royal Taster. At a medieval banquet, the king's food taster samples "the other white meat" and collapses before the assembled court. Pandemonium erupts. But it turns out he'd faked the poisoning so he could feast alone to his stomach's content. The spot, based on the fifty-second idea Bozell Worldwide presented to the NPPC, involved a huge crew and cast, elaborate costumes, a historically accurate set, months to make, and four different possible endings to keep the real one a secret.

Although NPPC savored the return on its Super Bowl investment, in

"ROYAL TASTER" The National Pork Producers Council cooked up a historical drama.

1998 it decided to use its marketing dollars in other venues to get into consumers' faces more often.

SELLING A HOT COMMODITY IN A COOL MEDIUM

Unless you drink a lot of Bloody Marys, you've probably had the same bottle of Tabasco in your cupboard for decades. (A little of this stuff goes a long way.) That's bad news for the McIlhenny family, who've been making the sauce deep in Louisiana Cajun country since 1865. But it was great news for Super Bowl fans. "Mosquito," which ran in local markets, attracted so much attention that the McIlhennys decided to show it at the following year's game.

"We wanted to say that it's cool before saying that it's hot," said Stephanie Dieste, account supervisor at DDB. "Mosquito" played to the image of Tabasco rather than illustrate the ways to use it, as prior ads had done. In 2000's "Comet" spot, meteors suddenly rain down on a Stonehenge-like scene, destroying everything in fiery explosions. The camera points upward. In the sky a god is watching TV, eating pizza, and—spilling his Tabasco pepper sauce.

"MOSQUITO" A young guy (actor Steve Monroe) on the front porch of his Bayou home douses his pizza with Tabasco. A hapless mosquito bites him and flies off, only to explode abruptly, as the man smiles wryly.

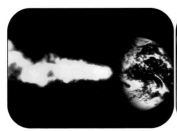  

"COMET" In Super Bowl XXXIV, having succeeded with "Mosquito," McIlhenny returned with more explosive stuff.

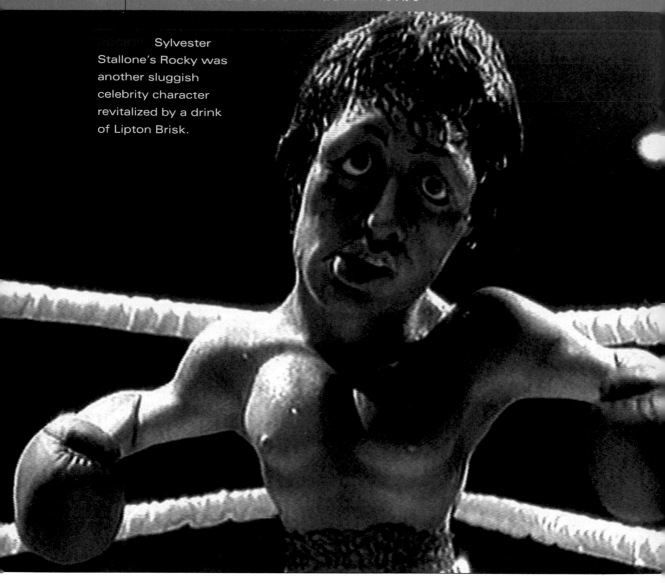

Sylvester Stallone's Rocky was another sluggish celebrity character revitalized by a drink of Lipton Brisk.

FOR YEARS COPARENTS PepsiCo and Unilever boldly promoted Lipton Brew and left low-end Lipton Brisk to fend for itself. Brisk fended fine, racking up brisk sales (which Brew never did). Impressed, in 1997 Lipton decided to see how Brisk would sell if it was supported by really cool ads.

Thus began an unusual Super Bowl challenge: to sell iced tea in winter. The commercials, created by JWT on miniature sets by a painstakingly slow stop-action process, featured stars, momentarily off their game, restored by Brisk. In commercial one, a true-to-life Claymation version of Frank Sinatra works up

"PLANET HOLLYWOOD" Wanting a display in Planet Hollywood, which Willis co-owns, the Jeffersons end up in a brawl with him.

"BABE" After Reggie Jackson offers Babe Ruth a Lipton Brisk, Ruth whacks a homer out of the stadium. (At the end, Ruth's bat flies from his hand, knocking over the Yankee club owner.)

a sweat performing, then retreats backstage to swill a "beyond cool" Brisk. The only color in the spot was his radiant blue eyes and sparkling blue Brisk can.

In 1998, an animated clay model of a hungover Babe Ruth swings wildly and moans he's "been up all night." A Claymation George Steinbrenner frets in the dugout; Reggie Jackson comes to the rescue, offering Babe a swig. "Ah, that's Brisk, baby!" says the legendary hitter.

A 1999 spot used Claymation models and the real voices of Bruce Willis and of Sherman Helmsley and Isabel Sanford from *The Jeffersons*.

Because reformulated Brisk tastes so good it can sell itself, in Super Bowl 2002 the Claymation director fires Danny DeVito and the spokespuppets, who riot.

"SPARKY" Fans loved Jason Alexander's Rold Gold adventure, where paratrooper Lloyd Bridges forced him out of a cargo transport plane.

JUST HOURS BEFORE SUPER BOWL 1995, Frito-Lay moved its extravagant $1.5 million Rold Gold pretzel commercial from halftime to the first quarter. In the spot, *Seinfeld* costar Jason Alexander looks like he's parachuting live into Joe Robbie Stadium, clutching "Sparky," played by the pooch from *Frasier*.

Instead, Frito-Lay had another halftime hit. New York and Texas ex-governors Mario Cuomo and Ann Richards empty out an office, musing about how tough it is to face change. "I should have seen it coming," Richards admits. "Maybe so, but now we ought to accept this change, embrace it…because change can be very exciting," Cuomo says. The change they're talking about turns out to be not the recent elections that ousted them, but the new Doritos Tortilla Chip bag.

Lineup changes are as common for the game's advertisers as for the players' bench. (The day before Super Bowl 1997, Frito-Lay canned its ad with comedian Chris Elliott bungee-jumping to dip a chip into salsa on the field, after a performer died practicing a similar stunt planned for that halftime.)

Extravaganzas are also common. Frito-Lay spent $20,000 a day to rent a C-130 military transport plane's fuselage for the Rold Gold spot; it appeared for mere seconds. "The name of the game is to make our news of the moment as big as it can be," said Brock Leach, former president of Frito-Lay's new-product group. Super Bowl Sunday is one of the year's top four "snacking occasions," along with July 4, Labor Day, and Memorial Day.

"Chips are fun, but they're not a serious product with serious brand loyalty commitment," said Charlie Miesmer, senior executive creative director at BBDO. In 1992,

"MARIO & ANN" Two govs who lost re-election bids bantered for Doritos. "Gee, Mario, both these teams are great. Too bad there can only be one winner," said Ann Richards. Cuomo snapped back, "Tell me about it."

Frito-Lay had improved its chip's taste, but "no one cares. We had to make them care." To do that, Miesmer roped in Larry Bird and Kareem Abdul-Jabbar.

BBDO modified "Betcha can't eat just one," the Lay's theme since 1963, to "Too good to eat just one." Abdul-Jabbar bet Bird he couldn't stop at one chip. Bird lost and ended up with a bald dome to match Kareem's (simulated by a skull cap).

Then came Super Bowl XXVIII. In Frito-Lay's most heralded spot, twelve-year-old Elijah Wood keeps bettering his seat at the game by winning the "eat-just-one bet," advancing with his bag of Wavy Lay's, ultimately displacing Dan Quayle in the front row and quarterback Troy Aikman on the Cowboys players' bench. With the same cheeky style and with no elaborate discussion of brand benefits, Frito-Lay scored a touchdown.

"REFRIGERATOR," above. In SB 1986, Jay Leno discussed "having a relationship" with Doritos, eating them at 2 A.M., and told parents where they should hide the chips that "taste as good as they crunch" from their kids. Here Jay Leno pens a shopping list for Doritos.

"GOOD EATER," above. Leno's Doritos ads encourage the crave: "Crunch all you want. We'll make more," they conclude.

"THE GUYS" Would Larry Bird fail to eat just one Tostito, as wagered by Kareem Abdul-Jabbar?

The year before, comedian Chevy Chase sped to rescue an oblivious chip-eating grandma from an approaching steamroller; instead, he saves the chips she's clutching. In 1994, in his first network appearance since Fox canceled his talk show, Chase spoofed his predicament. He's about to rescue an old lady stumbling in traffic, when a network bigwig yells, "Cut…Chevy, we gotta talk. You're canceled. It's ratings, demographics." At the end, the director consoles: "Chevy, keep the bag."

For its new Baked Lay's potato crisps, Frito-Lay turned to a star of a different ilk. Initially it sought to place porcine star Babe, the pig from the hit movie of the same name, poolside with supermodels Elle Macpherson, Vendela, Naomi Campbell, and Kathy Ireland to suggest you can root away and still be—what else?—a babe. But the starlet's handlers would have none of it. So Frito-

"PARTY" In Part One of a spot, former Dallas Cowboys coach Tom Landry, a real-life baldie, wagered NY Giants quarterback Phil Simms and linebacker Lawrence Taylor, Broncos quarterback John Elway, Raiders defensive end Howie Long and running back Eric Dickerson, and Bengals quarterback Boomer Esiason that they couldn't eat just one Lay's. Part Two showed he was right: They all appear bald.

"EXCUSE ME" A young Elijah Wood (later Frodo Baggins in *Lord of the Rings*) challenges his way into better seats, daring folks to eat just one chip. He bests Dan Quayle and Cowboys quarterback Troy Aikman.

"BRUCE" In 1994, Buffalo Bills' Bruce Smith couldn't restrain himself from indulging in chips and wound up wearing a dress.

"PARTY CHEVY" Chevy Chase lampooned the cancellation of his talk show for Tortilla Thins.

"LINE UP" In a 1996 spot, Miss Piggy hangs with the models chowing down Baked Lay's with no thought of their waistlines.

"LAUNDROMAT" In 1998, former Miss USA Ali Landry turns up the heat in a Laundromat for Doritos.

"LIBRARY" The following year, Landry munches new Doritos in the school library. The crunch is disquieting to the librarian in charge.

"MORE CHEESE" Ali Landry wins with Doritos on the tennis court, stoking the automatic ball server with the product.

"DREW'S PARTY" Drew Carey's 2001 Super Bowl party featured plenty of Doritos and retired quarterbacks comparing win-loss records.

Lay turned to the Muppet characters for an equally renowned pig—Miss Piggy.

But it was the use of "Doritos Girl" Ali Landry that really added sizzle. In a 1998 spot, Landry, a former Miss USA, saunters into a Laundromat in a tight white T-shirt. Two bug-eyed guys at the dryers stare, then perform tricks with their Doritos Puffs to impress her. The sultry siren one-ups them, extracting her chips from the dryer with kung fu and catching them while doing a split. "It's a shape you just want to eat," the narrator coos.

In the next Super Bowl, Landry is a coed munching new Doritos in the college library. The chips are so red-hot that she/they set off the fire alarm and sprinklers.

In 2001, she pours Doritos into the automatic ball machine, acing a star-struck young male tennis player. Yet in 2002, Doritos decided that online was a better way to reach teens who live there—and on snack food.

To make news in 2001, Frito-Lay rustled up comedian and television star Drew Carey to mock the win-loss records of John Elway and Jim Kelly. Retired quarterbacks play at Carey's Super Bowl party. Elway (2–3) wins big; Kelly goes down (0–4). Sales soared.

FOOD, FOLKS, AND FOOTBALL

Although McDonald's was on the big game from the start, for many years the chain sat on its buns, sidelined by the high costs or its own lack of "news." But when it did want to shout a message to the world, it used the Super Bowl as its megaphone.

In 1986, McDonald's was the biggest advertiser. It had something new to crow about: its new McDLT, a hot burger on one side and cold lettuce and tomato on the other. A pregame spot suggested great forces merging, by bringing together players from the Chicago Bears and New England Patriots. A postgame spot saluted the Bears with a "live" locker-room victory celebration. (Agency Leo Burnett had filmed both teams' locker rooms.)

In 1987, McDonald's wanted more retirees behind its counters. So it hired septuagenarian ex-sawmill owner Lowell Sexton as its "New Kid." In a Super Bowl spot, Sexton comes home from his first day on the job and proudly tells his similarly aged wife, "I don't know how they ever got along without me."

The following year, McD introduced its Cheddar Melt. Michael Jordan strolls into a McDonald's, the picture suddenly breaks up suggesting a transmission error, and stark white letters appear: "Quiet please. We have a pretty

"FOSSIL FUEL" The scent of McDonald's french fries awakens a T-rex.

"PERFECT SEASON" McDonald's touching spot with boys and their dads was voiced by actor Richard Dreyfuss.

"SWING" A baby's mood changes to happy each time her swing seat reaches the top of its arc and she sees McDonald's golden arches out the window.

"SHOWDOWN" "First one to miss watches the winner eat," Larry Bird taunts, eyeing Michael Jordan's Big Mac. Their shots start out easy enough—on one knee—but escalate into ludicrous dares until the two perch atop the John Hancock building across the expressway, aiming to put the ball "over the river, off the billboard, through the window, off the wall...nothing but net."

"NEW KID" McDonald's "New Kid" appealed to retirees.

important announcement. We were going to wait till halftime, but we were just too excited....McDonald's proudly announces the Cheddar Melt..." There was no sound throughout.

In 1990, McDonald's new "Food. Folks. Fun." campaign "restored the humanity that had been somewhat leeched by a barrage of price and game promotions and re-established this friendly, homey turf as ours," said Paul Shrage, then chief marketing officer. Americans had been out-slicked and out-advertised for so long that they hungered for basic human values, he said. McDonald's knew it had to make people feel as comfortable and as welcomed as an old friend. Shrage rejected witty spots in favor of emotion-tuggers. One spot chronicled a tyke's hard day at preschool. In another, a single mom shares job woes with her precocious daughter over a Happy Meal. "Perfect Season," the company's warm, fuzzy paean to Pee Wee football from Super Bowl 1992, showcased the real heroes—dads posing as goal posts. It reminded us that a good day wasn't determined by who won the game but by sharing the afternoon with muddy kids more interested in grasshoppers and McDonald's than gridiron strategy. Steven Spielberg hired the creators, Burnett's art director Bob Shallcross and copywriter Jim Ferguson, to develop it into a movie that became *Little Giants*.

McDonald's hoped to "trigger the crave" again with its wink-and-smile 1993 Super Bowl celebration of its long relationship with the NBA. In the tongue-in-cheeky "Showdown," superstar Larry Bird challenged Michael Jordan to play for Jordan's lunch—a Big Mac and fries.

For the next Super Bowl, Charles Barkley, Jordan's on-court rival and off-court buddy, wheedled his way into a rematch with even more preposterous shots "around

"FOOD, FOLKS, AND FUN" McDonald's "Food, Folks, and Fun" campaign re-established the brand on homey turf.

Saturn through the Big Dipper."

"Fossil Fuel," another animation tour de force, occurs inside a natural history museum at night. The bones of a giant tyrannosaurus stir to life, awakened by the intoxicating smell of McDonald's fries. The T-rex sets off to find them. When a dozing guard realizes that Dino wants his dinner, he playfully makes it do tricks, doling out fries as training bait.

"DID SOMEBODY SAY" "Did Somebody Say McDonald's" was back for Super Bowl XXXIV.

McD's 1996 Super Bowl spot aimed for understatement. An adorable infant coos and smiles when her swings rises, then whimpers when it swings away. A reverse cut shows what's causing her mood shift: She's overjoyed at spotting the golden arches above the window sill when her swing crests—and unhappy when they disappear from view. (No baby was harmed producing this spot: Rather she was filmed in all moods, and in postproduction the scenes were morphed.)

Americans cheered "Swing," a Hong Kong version used a Chinese baby, and Arby's copied it showing a guy on a porch swing reacting the same way to its sign. But all the attention failed to stem a market-share slide that year for McD's.

Wounded by such mid-'90s blunders as the Arch Deluxe sandwich and Campaign 55 discount program, McDonald's sat out Super Bowls 1996 through 1999. In 2000, it served up a rendition of its then-two-year-old "Did Somebody Say McDonald's?" theme. Its 2002 Super Bowl commercial reminded viewers of their real values. A gap-toothed kid runs in the rain to catch a descending football, then revels with food and fries in McDonald's as a voice wonders: "Did he catch it? Does it matter?"

"The Super Bowl isn't a time when consumers want to know how much a Big Mac costs," said Burnett's Cheryl Berman. "They want to be entertained here, to see the best of the best."

Financial services
companies know the
buck stops here. To sell
financial services, ad
agencies have to make
investing and insurance
tangible on television.
That challenge has led
to some touching and
well-remembered spots.

10

MONEY PLAYS

MEN ARE THE GENDER most associated with money. So it's no surprise that all manner of financial purveyors flocked to the Super Bowl ad venue to address them.

For years, banks had positioned themselves as good neighbors with warm, fuzzy ads. First Union Corp. took a decidedly different tack.

After it had morphed from a regional financier into a veritable colossus owning CoreStates Financial and The Money Store, First Union wanted notice for its reformation. "Financial World" in Super Bowl XXXIII (1999) was its vehicle. The dark, disturbing vision featured a hellish, bizarre urban landscape of financial manholes, negotiable only with First Union's help. Faceless people in trench coats and bowler hats trudge down rain-soaked streets, past fire-breathers, fortune-tellers, and painted-faced freaks. Everything is made of money or monetary symbols. Little red cars (representing debt) dart around long black ones (representing solvency). Things smash, topple over, shatter. In another spot, sharks swim with crocodiles in a partly submerged, decrepit bank vault.

"This is a world of risk and uncertainty, where the roads can take you to success or prosperity—or, sometimes, to no place at all. This is the financial world." The ominous voice belongs to Hal Riney of Hal Riney & Partners, architect of the campaign.

111

"NOISE" First Union launched a surreal campaign, urging customers to move to the bank for all their financial services.

"For decades, banks and investment firms of mountainous size have ruled the land. Yet high above the horizon, another mountain has risen—a mountain called First Union, with sixteen million customers, the nation's eighth-largest brokerage and sixth-largest bank." A gleaming glass-and-steel mountain emblazoned with its name emerges, along with an invitation to "come to a mountain called First Union. Or, if you prefer, the mountain will come to you."

"We were frustrated that we were one of the fifteen largest financial institutions, and no one knew our name," said Jim Garrity, senior VP of brand management and now executive vice president and chief marketing officer of Wachovia. After the Super Bowl, everyone did.

But many didn't like what they knew. They felt that the fast-paced campaign was eye-catching but chaotic, extravagant at its $100 million cost, and ultimately misguided. The images were dark when America's mood and economy were not, and the looming corporate monolith represented what people fear and loathe in financial institutions. They saw First Union as the bank from hell. In 2001, First Union bought Wachovia and kept Wachovia's name, nullifying both the good and bad of much of its ad investment.

"E.T." In a 1999 halftime commercial for Progressive Auto Insurance, E.T. returns to his spaceship to report about life on Earth. Conditions are good overall, he reports, but humans rush around in cars and have accidents.

IT SEEMED LIKED A SURE THING in the insurance world where risk is the lifeblood. Progressive Auto Insurance invested $20 million in SB XXXIII (1999) picturing E.T. as a "safety ambassador." The space critter was a well-known, beloved metaphor for healing, and advertising on the Super Bowl was, although pricey, a surefire way to attract attention. Progressive yearned for that, and to change what little image it did have from that of a company focused on high-risk drivers to one that covers all motorists.

People liked the E.T. commercial, but it didn't drive them to Progressive as

"BILL HEATER" John Hancock's "Real Life. Real Answers." campaign used a cinema verité style to show everyday people and simple financial solutions.

Chairman Peter B. Lewis had anticipated. Soon after, he fired the Arnell agency that crafted the campaign. They sued Progressive for unpaid invoices and damages, claiming personal connections had obtained rights to license E.T. Luckily the extraterrestrial had already gone home.

THE IDEA FOR JOHN HANCOCK struck them at a neighborhood bar. During one of their many problem-solving walks around Boston's Back Bay, Bill Heater, a copywriter at the Hill, Holliday, Connors, Cosmopulos agency and his partner, art director Don Easdon, stopped in for a beer, overheard real conversations, and hit upon the "Real Life. Real Answers." campaign. It was the early 1980s. The venerable John Hancock Financial Services Co. was under siege from banks and brokerages nibbling at its asset base. Hancock now offered all manner of financial services—and wanted all manner of prospects to know. It needed to come up with something as powerful as its once relevant "Put your John Hancock on a John Hancock" song and as solid as Prudential's rock, Allstate's cupped hands, MetLife's Snoopy character, and Travelers' umbrella. A documentary film on the Loud family, a 1973 precursor to the 21st-century reveal-all Osbournes, had had a big impact on TV a decade earlier. Easdon and Heater decided to show everyday folks, like those in the bar, in documentary-style dramas built around emotionally charged, life-changing events, like a baby's birth. Unlike competitors that promoted what they could do for you or relied on feel-good symbols, Hancock's emotional dramas would grip the head and heart by combining reality with sentimentality.

They videotaped a spot of Heater rocking his infant daughter to sleep. Type on a screen presents his dossier ("Bill Heater, 30, married, two children, income $35,000") as dad coos, "I love you, little Jenny Katherine. I've got something very, very important to tell you. Daddy got a raise." (Pause.) "Are you listening?"

Subsequently, his estimated expenses (income tax, rent, food, etc.) flash ledger-style on the screen. "That means, uh, that I can buy you a sandbox, playhouse…. It means I can buy you a sliding board, a little bicycle, a diamond ring." Envisioning a mink coat, he decides that "maybe we should put some of it away." Screen text provides the "answer": John Hancock's five investment options and the "Real Life. Real Answers." tag line. The "spec" ad snagged the account for the agency and became the first commercial in the campaign.

Subsequent spots featured characters so real you'd swear they weren't actors, bearing names of actual agency employees and financial dossiers that were composites of Hancock policyholders. Kevin Driscoll mused nocturnally to his half-asleep wife about his dreams to work for himself someday. The screen text shows some suggestions to accumulate capital for his new business while protecting his investments. One vignette showed a twenty-six-year-old bachelor, who earns $30,000 a year and spends

$27,000, being upbraided for fiscal irresponsibility by his brother. And, in another spot, Margaret and Tom Fitzgerald let their anxieties brim over at the closing ceremony of buying their first home. The actors mumbled and shrugged, looked away, and spoke over each other, and their voices were immersed in background noise to suggest we really were eavesdropping on actual families working out financial plans. Heater described the style as "newsy and nosy." What they were, in fact, were hard-sell ads served up in the softest, most palatable way.

Oddly, field agents initially found them too low-key. There was no pitch. The name John Hancock was never spoken and didn't appear in the script until near the end. President David D'Alessandro overruled them. After the commercial was widely praised, agents rallied behind it. Later it was adapted to print ads. "Real Life. Real Answers." ran for ten years, although on the Super Bowl only through XXII (1988).

"JON AND DANA REVISITED"
Lovitz and Carvey pay by plastic—the no-spending limit AmEx card, accepted everywhere. The other card is spurned everywhere except at a schlocky souvenir stand.

"BURRO" Visa showed two tourists in an Italian town who unwittingly trade their camera for a burro. Luckily, they can replace it because they carry Visa Gold.

IN THE 1960S, long before we carried around eight to ten credit cards (and when debit cards hadn't yet been invented), the purveyors of plastic had discovered the big game. American Express was first, but Visa muscled it aside, eventually becoming the exclusive charge card of Super Bowl XXIII.

Even so, Visa didn't buy time in that 1989 game, leaving the path clear for American Express to tweak its adversary. AmEx teamed with *Saturday Night Live* buddies Dana Carvey and Jon Lovitz on a road trip to Robbie Stadium.

AmEx won that round, but Visa was winning the war celebrating places like Rosalie's in Marblehead, Massachusetts, where "they don't take no for an answer and they don't take American Express. Visa: It's everywhere you want to be." That punch line tied Visa to acceptability, while distinguishing it from MasterCard. It shattered the widely held perception that Visa and Master-Card are interchangeable, said Jan Soderstrom, former executive vice president of marketing for Visa International.

In a Super Bowl 1994 Visa ad, two tourists in quaint medieval Todi, Italy, try to get locals to snap their photo with the boys' burro. The boys think the tourists want to make a trade, so delightedly take the camera and leave the donkey. Luckily,

"DREAM TEAM" "Dream Team" Olympian Hakeem Olajuwon treats a rival team to lunch with the Visa Gold card.

"THEY'RE COMING" Visa also went for the giggle. Foreigners try to learn a Southern dialect in time for the Atlanta summer Olympics.

the tourists are carrying Visa Gold and can replace their camera.

In 1995, Visa was facing increased competition and a new consumer interest in value over status. Subtle changes resulted. Instead of a French château (used in 1986), Visa showed its card proffered at a hamburger joint and the circus. It also touted its association with big events like Paul McCartney's tour, the U.S. Open, and the 1996 Olympics.

The next year, MasterCard played here for the first time. In one spot, a pilot from the Outback buys a sandwich with a smart card. In another, a forger in a subterranean lair is foiled by MasterCard's technology. Soon after, MC abandoned "Smart Money." "It was too focused on benefits and not enough on an emotional connection," said marketing vice president Larry Flanagan. In 1997, McCann-Erickson coined "There are some things money can't buy. For everything else, there's MasterCard." The "Priceless" campaign was born. At last, after several ineffective campaigns, MasterCard had fuel to fight Visa.

"Priceless" compared the monetary costs of hot dogs and tickets at a baseball game with the priceless benefits: "Real conversation with eleven-year-old son." Christmas gifts for a toddler were compared with the priceless experience of "watching her play with the cardboard box." Viewers liked the spots, remembered them, and used MasterCard more often.

"BASEBALL" MasterCard's "Priceless" campaign highlighted the things money can't buy.

"DEION" Clerks and customers fawn over pro footballer Deion Sanders, but he can't buy athletic gear with a check. He needs the Visa check card.

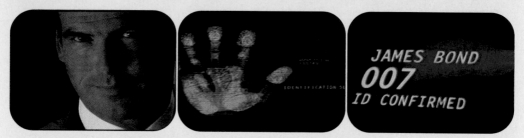

"JAMES BOND" James Bond (Pierce Brosnan) has passed a security system via voice, handprint, and corneal scan, but can't buy caviar at a Secret Service snack bar without ID.

"SHIRLEY" Even though a shopkeeper has shared past lives with Shirley MacLaine, without the Visa check card the actress must show ID to pay by check.

VISA'S CHECK CARD

Visa ruled, albeit over a relatively small kingdom. In 1979, cash and checks paid for 75 percent of personal expenditures. Gradually, resistance to Visa's new check or debit card lessened, and in 1995 Visa went all-out to woo people away from paper. A debut campaign introduced Ray and Earl, two codgers relaxing on a porch; one just received a Visa check card and explains to his friend how it works.

"DAFFY DUCK" Daffy Duck gets the same "no-ID" brush-off at the Warner Bros. Studio store.

"BOB DOLE" Even in his home-town, Bob Dole is hassled to prove his identity. Better get a Visa check card.

"NIGEL" If only the palace guard had used a Visa check card to pay the dry cleaner.

By Super Bowl XXXI (1997), use of Visa's check cards had mushroomed. Visa tapped someone unmistakable to maintain its trajectory. Bob Dole was a traditional, old-world guy using a new-world pay system—an approach designed to convert remaining doubters. The presidential candidate returns home to Russell, Kansas, where crowds host a welcome parade. But when he tries to pay by check for lunch at the town diner, the waitress demands driver's license, passport, military ID, voter card. A voice-over suggests trying Visa

"VACUUM" Like the nozzle that sucks up her annoying boyfriend, Visa is the right tool for the right job.

"ELEPHANT" A dad buys his daughter her dream elephant with his Visa card.

check card. "It automatically deducts from your checking account. No ID needed." Dole mutters the last word: "I just can't win."

Visa continued to tickle the next year with Nigel. A Buckingham Palace guard must stand immobile and suffer through discomfort and indignity wearing plain clothes because the dry cleaner holding his uniform wouldn't take a check.

Visa proved it could also tug at the heartstrings in a commercial about a little girl who yearns for a pet elephant, and a doting dad whose Visa card brings her fantasy to life. The child plaintively imagines doing headstands side by side with her pet pachyderm. "You may not be able to give her everything her heart desires," begins a voice-over. "Then again…maybe you can." As the radiant daughter hugs her new stuffed toy, the voice adds: "And besides, you never know what she'll want next." The girl then walks off with a live zebra.

"'Elephant' stood apart from the usual in-your-face humor of the game and symbolized every wish that's bigger than it can be," said BBDO copywriter (now senior executive creative director) Jimmy Siegel.

"REAL LIFE" Comedian Jerry Seinfeld searches for a real life in American Express commercials.

Meanwhile, AmEx was still playing the celebrity card. In Super Bowl XXXII (1998), spokesman Jerry Seinfeld teamed with his animated idol, Superman, to rescue Lois Lane, who's forgotten her wallet at the grocer. (Seinfeld claimed he wrote his own ads.)

In 1999, it was a three-way card-fight. While searching for his "real life" after leaving his old show, Seinfeld visits Mt. Rushmore, holds scalding coffee, mutters, frets about wolves, can't feel his face, chats with a willowy blonde, punches the St. Louis

"BACON" Visa plays six degrees of Kevin Bacon with the man himself.

Arch, and drives to the Big Apple—continuing the nothingness of his show.

In a "Priceless" MasterCard cartoon, Mr. Magoo needs contacts ($320); Yogi Bear, a treadmill ($800); and Olive Oyl, a Wonderbra ($26). The priceless component: "Being happy with who you are," expressed by Fred Flintstone.

Meanwhile Visa, with a 53 percent share of the $1.16 trillion card category, turned to overly zealous fans. An expectant mom scours a paint store for the perfect shade of orange, not, it turns out, for baby's room but to paint her face Denver Broncos' colors.

That acerbic touch got stronger the following year. A sloppy guy in a dirty undershirt, watching a cartoon on TV and picking popcorn from his teeth, points out a spot his girlfriend missed while trying out the new vacuum. She points the nozzle at *him,* sucking him up. "It really does work," she muses. And we're reminded that Visa is the right tool for the right job.

And in 2001 at a snooty auction house, the letter "B" ("used by Shakespeare and Cookie Monster"), the color red ("stops cars and causes bulls to charge"), and gravity ("paperweight of the cosmos") are being bid on. "For everything else, there's MasterCard."

The next year, Visa had the stage to itself. It reminded us we couldn't buy Olympics, Triple Crown, or NASCAR tickets without Visa, and did a riff from the "Six Degrees of Kevin Bacon" game. When a clerk asks the actor for ID so he can cash a check, an ID-less Bacon corrals a doctor, a priest, and others to verify who he is. Alas, even the six-person chain between himself and the cashier can't do what the card does.

When a huge audience expects the unexpected, it's worth taking some risks to deliver that. But sometimes an ad's clever fake-out play doesn't get past the viewers' defense zone.

11

SOME SURPRISING PLAYS

IN HIS FORTY-PLUS YEARS in Hollywood, Fred Astaire danced with a mop, a hat-stand, canes, golf clubs, chairs, and Ginger Rogers. But before Super Bowl XXXI (1997), he'd never partnered with a vacuum cleaner. Royal Appliance Manufacturing doctored clips from *Royal Wedding* and *Easter Parade,* in which Astaire had two-stepped with a coat-rack and cane, to show him cheek-to-nozzle with a Dirt Devil Broom Vac. After the digital twirl, sales picked up, but Astaire's fans lambasted his widow, Robyn, for commercializing his legend.

Mars has long known that kids were its biggest fans yet lacked the cash to buy M&M's. So Mars sold moms on a rational benefit: "Melts in your mouth, not in your hand." And it sold everyone on stories that poked fun at itself.

Its early chocolate-covered animations were pleasant but passive mnemonic devices. After BBDO won its business in 1995, they became more anthropomorphic and irreverent, empathy-inducing protagonists in constant danger of being eaten.

Red was a calculating, boastful attention-seeker; Yellow, a good-hearted, trusting simpleton. Green became the first femme fatale M&M's in 1997, promoting her autobiography, *I Melt for No One.* Blue is wry, understated, occasionally sarcastic. Convincing Mars to make M&M's small-minded, hostile, spiteful, and dopey was

"MYTH" Comedian Dennis Miller asks the pouty-lipped confection if it's "true what they say about green M&M's?" She looks shocked and defensive.

necessary to make an emotional connection with the consumer, but no easy matter, admitted BBDO's Charles Miesmer.

Several spots on Super Bowl XXXI played up the old myth that green M&M's are aphrodisiacs. Mars mischievously feigned ignorance.

In Super Bowl 2000, Green saunters down the street to a volley of catcalls. Then, in 2001, the movie star with bedroom eyes has her shell off when her producer walks in on her in her star trailer.

M&M's began milking its Roman numeral–like name and its status as "The Official Candy of the New Millennium" with four spots in XXXII (1998). In one, Red and Yellow tell everyone in Rome that M&M stands for the year 2000. They try to get a Mars official to create a billboard, but wind up erecting it themselves—during a lightning storm. The next year (SB XXXIII), four "Oh, no! They're gonna eat Crispy!" ads introduced a 3D computer-generated baby character.

In one spot, the orange-shelled chocolate lolls in a swimming pool repelling the advances of Halle Berry by warning of the dangers of swimming on a full stomach. In another ad, Crispy (in baby booties) flings himself to the floor to ward off actor Patrick Warburton (Puddy on *Seinfeld*). "Can't eat a candy that fell on the floor," Crispy snips. The lug looming over him deadpans, "Why? Whose rule?"

The human–candy interaction offered more laughs in Super Bowl XXXVI (2002) to get people to think M&M's when they think chocolate. The check-in clerk at a fancy hotel asks a weary traveler if he'd like a chocolate on his pillow at bedtime. Instead of the inanimate mint found in traditional turndown service, the guest finds neurotic Red on the bed asking, "Mind if I watch TV?"

"TRAILER" Green, in her on-location star trailer, gets caught with her shell off.

"LIFEGUARD" Having fun with Halle Berry, Orange backs away to save himself from being eaten.

"HOTEL" Mars plumped its curmudgeonly M&M's Red on the pillow of an unsuspecting hotel guest who'd requested a bedtime chocolate.

"WE" Red and Yellow create a billboard during a lightning storm.

M&M's may deliver for Mars, but Snickers is its sweetest seller. In late 1996 and on through the 2000 Super Bowl, Mars tried to encourage viewers to grab one with hilarious "Not going anywhere for a while?" ads.

In "Team Prayer," a coach enlists a swarm of religious leaders to ensure that the pregame prayers are politically correct. In "Chefs," a worker finally finishes painting the team's name on the field only to find he's written "Chefs," not "Chiefs." While "Chefs" didn't run on the game, the takeoff, "Clarence," did, in 1997. This time the same hapless worker is stuck in the ice at a hockey rink.

"CHEFS" Misspelling "Chiefs" means the field worker might need a Snickers bar for a snack while he repaints the end zone. A successor ad was used on the Super Bowl.

Then in 2001, Mars launched Snickers Cruncher on Super Bowl Sunday XXXV with funny vignettes showing people relieving frustration by crunching something. In one such spot, "Car Alarm," a woman pushes a sofa out of her window to silence a grating car alarm below. That evolved to focus on mistakes people make when they're hungry.

AFTER YEARS OF USING local testimonials in its ads, in 1996 Mail Boxes Etc. ventured onto the Super Bowl, forking over a good chunk of its annual ad budget to ride Oscar Mayer's coattails. During halftime, the Wienermobile driver described how MBE serves as his "office on the road."

Recognizing that the bulk of its customers are small business owners, in 1997 Mail Boxes Etc. highlighted some in its new "Making Business Easier Worldwide" ads. It also launched a "See Your Small Business on the Super Bowl" search. In 1998, the company received 3,500-plus entries from small businesses eager to be on the big game. Alaska-based Wilderness Air, which used an MBE office to ship salmon, won the $10,000 prize and fifteen seconds of fame. In 1999, Jeremy Kraus, founder of Jeremy's Microbatch Ice Creams, won MBE's second contest while still

"POCKET PUMP" This low-budget commercial-within-a-commercial featuring Chuck and Rob, inventors of a basketball-inflating Pocket Pump, was so successful that customers urged Mail Boxes Etc. to repeat it.

in college by applying the trendy idea of microbreweries to ice cream. Although the media wrote about these small fries thrust into the big time, Mail Boxes Etc. (since acquired by UPS) abandoned the Bowl after 1999.

MASTER LOCK: THE MOUSE THAT ROARED

In June 1998, Master Lock ran the first nationally broadcast 1-second commercial: a bullet pierces a Master Lock, which shudders but holds fast. That blink-and-you'd-miss-it moment was enough to telegraph the message. Master Lock's signature image had become embedded in the American psyche during twenty-one Super Bowl appearances.

Since it shelled out just $107,000 to run on the Super Bowl in 1974—a voice announced that a sharpshooter at a firing range was sighting in on its #15 lock—Master Lock has shot holes in thousands of locks. The primary target was not consumers but distributors, recalled Greg Clausen, executive vice president and director of media at Cramer-Krasselt, Master Lock's agency. Yet consumers heeded the call. In 1974, the company had annual sales of $220 million, more than 70 percent market share, and almost universal brand recognition.

After four years, the suspense of whether the lock could sustain the

"LOCK ABUSE" Lock things in or lock them out, Master Lock played up its image for standing up to abuse in 1978.

"MARKSMAN" Master Lock built its reputation for selling a "blast-proof" lock. Ads showed it standing up to a rifle's best effort.

CAESARS PALACE　　　HOOVER DAM　　　ELY MAXIMUM SECURITY PRISON

"SECURITY MATTERS" Who counts on Master Lock for safety? One ad touted real clients Caesars Palace, Hoover Dam, and Ely Maximum Security Prison.

marksman's shot had ebbed. In 1978, the "Tough Under Fire" theme with the Master Lock bouncing like Superman's chest while deflecting a rifle blast became its signature. Master Lock boasted that its product could "lock in, lock out, lock up, or lock down almost anything" and showed it—securing a bike, strongbox, locker, and tiger in a cage.

"Each year the Super Bowl was the cornerstone of our marketing program. Each year we felt like we'd won the game," says James H. Beardsley, who retired as CEO of Master Lock in 1997.

Beardsley's team bet big on the Bowl, which devoured its yearly marketing budget. Before each game Master Lock reminded hardware wholesalers that by building a brand, they justified charging a premium price—and people would willingly pay. In 1994, commercials took Super Bowl viewers on a fast-paced tour of "places where security matters most": the Hoover Dam, Caesars Palace, Ely Maximum Security Prison in Nevada, and a Wells Fargo Armored Service truck in Houston. All really do use Master Locks. The images were intercut with scary shots of a man slowly pulling bullets from a rack, methodically loading them and firing (ineffectually) into a Master Lock.

In its Super Bowl swan song (1996), Master Lock mixed dark, brooding images of ominous back alleys, dangerous-looking men, and frightening crime scenes with unsettling lyrics from "For What It's

"SOMETHING'S HAPPENING HERE" As Master Lock's ads got darker and more frightening, the company felt they fell out of synch with the Super Bowl's festive atmosphere.

ONLY MASTER LOCK BETWEEN YOU AND THIS TIGER

Worth," Stephen Stills/Buffalo Springfield's 1960s anthem of alienation. "There's something happening here; What it is ain't exactly clear. There's a man with a gun over there, Telling me I gotta beware…" The implication was that crime is random and unpredictable and that a Master Lock provides a sense of security.

But by then, the landscape had changed. Competition and the cost of raw materials were rising, while crime and Master Lock's share were dropping. And critics questioned how padlocks could protect people from modern predators.

"We needed to make this a lifestyle purchase, not a hardware purchase," admitted Beardsley. The Super Bowl no longer seemed the ideal place to do that, or to launch new products to targeted niches—like neon-colored locks for kids, marine products, and gunlocks. "We were costed out and cluttered out," recalls John Melamed, senior vice president at Cramer-Krasselt. The game didn't jive with Master Lock's key purchase time, back-to-school season, or key audience—women who buy their kids new locks to replace lost ones or forgotten combinations.

When Master Lock announced in early 1997 that it had retired from the Super Bowl, it garnered more media attention with that one statement than if it had advertised—without shelling out a penny.

IT'S ONE THING for an ad to strike out when it's aired on *Hollywood Squares;* it's quite another to flop when the world is watching. A Super Bowl ad is under a microscope from start to finish "with everyone waiting for it to tank, and to rip it to shreds," says Jimmy Siegel, executive vice president of BBDO.

For some advertisers, the spills are nasty. Steve Hayden, who wrote Apple's "1984" and "Lemmings" commercials, said, "We christened the Super Bowl as *the* venue for great ads…and for great, historic flops."

Just for Feet suffered a case of foot-in-mouth disease in XXXIII. The year before, in 1998, Just for Feet's new agency, Saatchi & Saatchi, had proposed that the retailer go for broke on the Super Bowl in its first national branding effort. CEO Harold Ruttenberg leapt at the chance to spend $1.7 million for a third-quarter spot to build goodwill. They concocted a contest around the ad and shelled out $2 million to promote it.

In "Kenyan," four military officials in a Humvee track a barefoot runner as if he were an animal. They offer him water—laced with a knockout drug—and after he drinks and collapses, unconscious, they force new Nikes onto his feet. The Kenyan (he wears a national team jersey) awakens horrified and tries to kick off the shoes. "We're Just for Feet, to preserve and protect feet," a narrator concluded.

The commercial (which was actually filmed in California using a Ghanaian runner) got bumped to the fourth quarter and was quickly vilified. *Ad Age* called it "neo-colonialist, culturally imperialist, probably racist" and "certainly condescending" and questioned the sanity of its creators. *The New York Times* called it "appallingly insensitive." *The Des Moines Register* said it "makes Denny's and Texaco look like abolitionists" and suggested shackling those who conceived it.

Saatchi called it a humorous spoof on how Just for Feet employees can be so passionate about their jobs that they sometimes do the wrong thing. JFF called it "stupid" and "politically incorrect" and likened itself to a patient who goes in for a nose job and finds the doctor has removed a lung.

Just for Feet sued Fox for moving the spot to the fourth quarter, nullifying its costly promotion, and refused to pay Saatchi's $3 million fee. Saatchi sued to collect and JFF countersued for $10 million, citing advertising malpractice. Just for Feet presented itself as a marketing country bumpkin, submissive to Saatchi's imperious creative team. Ruttenberg claimed that he had asked for a fun, noncontroversial ad and that upon seeing it shortly before the Super Bowl, he was horrified. Saatchi, he said, reassured him that it was brilliant and break-through. The case settled privately, and in November 2000 Just for Feet filed for Chapter 11 bankruptcy protection.

NO HOTEL CHAIN IS BETTER KNOWN than Holiday Inn. But with an old-gray-mare image, it was hard to compete with the Hiltons, Marriotts, and Sheratons out there. So in 1996, the company hired Fallon McElligott to change that image by focusing on its $1 billion renovation.

Days before the 1997 Super Bowl, John Sweetwood, Holiday Inn's market-ing chief at the time, promised "a wake-up call...a fun, attention-grabber." Boy, did he deliver. A voluptuous woman turns heads as she strides through a twentieth-year class reunion. A voice-over recites the cost of her bodily enhancements, including a nose job and breast implants. She greets an old classmate who never forgets a face; he cringes as he realizes he's looking at the former Bob Johnson. "It's amazing, the changes you can make for a few thou-sand dollars. Imagine what Holiday Inn will look like when we spend a billion," adds the voice-over.

Even though the spot contained no call to action or even an 800 number, franchisees overwhelmingly liked him/her. Viewers did not. The Southern Baptist Convention's Home Mission Board, for one, complained loudly about its gender-bending content. Others grumbled that this apple pie, Middle American brand had swished out of character. Two days later, Holiday Inn bowed to pressure and shelved the spot.

IN 1967, WHEN CHRISTOPHER REEVE was fourteen and doing his first com-mercial for a $10 J. C. Penney dress shirt, he overheard a director tell some-one to "do something with that kid's bland face." Three decades later, John Nuveen & Company did. They digitally attached the adult Reeve's head to an ambulatory body for a Super Bowl 2000 commercial.

At an awards banquet in the near future, an announcer celebrates how medical ills have been eradicated—including paralysis—as he presents an award to the immobile star of *Superman*. As music soars and Reeve rises and walks across a stage, a tag line flashes: "Leave your mark." Viewers squirmed, appalled by a spot they labeled maudlin, crass, and exploitative. It might have worked for a hospital medical website or public service spot, some claimed, but not for an investment company.

PETS.COM'S WHITE-AND-BROWN tube sock with mismatched eyes became the poster pup of the dot-com days, urging humans to shop online "because pets can't drive." The e-tailer spent $2 million on a spot in Super Bowl 2000 in which the sock carried a mike and crooned "Don't Go." An owner leaves his real dog in the garage as he drives away to the Chicago song "If You Leave Me Now," moving a zoo-full of animals to tears.

The playful puppet broke through the clutter and struck a chord with consumers, but all its barking couldn't overcome intense competition and high shipping costs. In November 2000, Pets.com shut down.

WHEN IT ABSOLUTELY, POSITIVELY HAS TO SPARKLE

In 1973, soon after Federal Express began shuttling packages in the dead of night, it began running some of the wittiest, most engaging ads around.

Research convinced FedEx that speed of delivery wasn't all that mattered. More important to customers was the security that what they sent would get there. That insight led to "When it absolutely, positively has to be there overnight."

After watching balding, mustachioed John Moschitta perform his fast-talking specialty on the television show *That's Incredible* in 1981, a team at Ally & Gargano concocted the character Spleen, who spews into an intercom at 450 words a minute to mimic the pace at which FedEx operated. "Helloooo Federal" and other ads made America roar, albeit

"HIDING" Although it never ran in the Super Bowl, this thigh-slapper from BBDO showed typical FedEx wit. In it, harried employee Sprizter hid because the package he sent never reached Albuquerque.

"APPLAUSE" In a revenge-of-the-working-girl spot in 1993, a tyrannical boss shuffles off after being shown he'd signed for his missing package. Her cowering colleagues wildly applaud her.

nervously, about wimpy employees and incompetent executives.

Some situations were close to real life, but the characters enacting them were hilarious caricatures. Take Bingham, who "sent the blueprints to Birmingham for the big meeting tomorrow" that was to be held in Binghamton.

By 1996, FedEx had gone global. Fearing humor didn't travel well, it got serious. FedEx's "the way the world works" spots from BBDO told of entrepreneurs around the world—like a publisher in Wales whose pop-up books thrilled children in Thailand—helped by FedEx's deliveries and warehousing.

FedEx's funny bone was not long stilled, however. In Super Bowl XXXII (1998), a fictitious company scrolls an apology across a test pattern of color bars: Its real commercial with dancing kangaroos and Garth Brooks couldn't

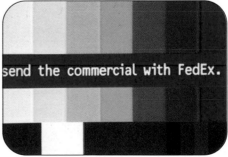

"RED ALERT" In 1996, in FedEx's first Super Bowl appearance, an overstressed boss with a tight deadline and an office full of materials to ship yells, "Red Alert," only to find that a savvy secretary has already called FedEx.

"APOLOGY" In FedEx's 1998 ad, the conceit was that the "real" ad absolutely, positively didn't arrive, because someone failed to send it via FedEx—hence the test pattern.

"BOLIVIA" In 1999, in another of FedEx's "mix-up" spots, the victorious Detroit Red Wings hockey team and chanting fans impatiently await the arrival of the Stanley Cup at the Joe Louis Arena. Instead, some cut-rate delivery service shows up—with a bag of burro food. Meanwhile, the Cup is delivered to a Bolivian farmer—by the name of José Luis Arena—who can't feed the trophy to his donkeys.

"LAUNCH" In SB XXXV (2001), a maker of reclining chairs is forced to install heavy-duty springs—with hilarious results—when his resupply of light-duty ones doesn't arrive.

run, the voice explains, because "some boob" from its (now ex-) ad agency didn't use FedEx to send it to NBC.

A spot on the 2000 game caused a stir. FedEx mixed clips from *The Wizard of Oz* with images of its truck delivering helium-filled balloons to Munchkins, whose hoarse voices regain their high pitch once they inhale the gas. The National Inhalant Prevention Coalition protested that the ad sent the wrong message, and FedEx subsequently squelched it.

In 2001, "This is a job for FedEx" replaced the two-year old "Be absolutely sure" tag line. To tout its extended hours, at a formal dinner a CEO credits his staff's "professionalism and poise" for his success, just as a junior employee, rushing a package to FedEx, tumbles off a balcony onto a guest table. He presses on frantically to the FedEx office. "Wanna stop rushing to make shipping cutoffs?" a voice-over asks. "Introducing FedEx extra hours." Despite being bloodied by the economy, FedEx bought time in the big game in 2002, albeit to run an old Dilbertesque concept.

FedEx Super Bowl commercials have been more than gimmicks. They've consistently and adroitly given wing to this brand.

"GREAT IDEA" Execs sit around a table discussing ways to cut costs. An underling proposes using FedEx. His swinish boss makes the suggestion his own, pitching it with a different hand gesture.

It might be a Noah's ark, or a sizzling sauna. Advertisers have used both beauty and beasts to stimulate sales.

12

MONKEY BUSINESS: SEX AND ANIMALS

IT'S NO SECRET THAT SEX SELLS. But Victoria's Secret went beyond sexy to border on indecent exposure in its 1999 Super Bowl debut.

The commercial was an outgrowth of Victoria's Secret's website and intended to make women smile, men take notice, and everyone log on for an online fashion show. Nancy Kramer, founder of Resource Marketing, reasoned that while 90 percent of Victoria's Secret shoppers are women, strutting its stuff on the game eleven days before Valentine's Day would draw men in and dramatically expand its audience. (It worked: The audience for the fashion show a few days later rivaled the one that watched the release of President Clinton's videotaped appearance before the grand jury. Men subsequently accounted for 35 percent of Victoria's Secret's online sales.)

"The two Super Bowl teams won't be there, but you won't care," the ad teased before showing lace-trimmed jiggle from its 1998 fashion show.

Ed Razek, president of creative services for parent Intimate Brands, dismissed complaints about titillation for titillation's sake, snapping that Victoria's Secret wasn't using lingerie to sell trucks, tortillas, or tonic. "If anybody has a right to use lingerie to sell lingerie, it's us. It would be criminal if we didn't."

Westin Hotels & Resorts likewise teased at naughtiness in its first global cam-

"INTERNET" Come-hither Victoria's Secret models traipsed and shimmied down the runway, shaking their bra-and-panty-clad booties to build viewership for an upcoming webcast.

paign, with spots in the big game. "Other hotel marketers tend to show beaches, lobby shots, and bellmen dancing," said Marc Pujalet, who was Westin's senior marketing vice president. "We're showing the customer and the reason why he stays with us. It's a nontraditional approach that's more like a beverage or fragrance ad in focusing on the experience that reflects the consumer's self-image."

In one Westin spot, a woman's sultry voice notes the guy "broke his neck to get the job, then broke the corporate sales record. Even broke the corporate no-jeans rule. Who's he sleeping with?" The narrator concludes urging viewers to "choose your travel partner wisely."

Norwegian Cruise Line was looking to sell the emotional experience of cruising, rather than more rational considerations, in 1994. The company's new president, Adam Aron, initially ordered Goodby, Silverstein to get steamy. "All people want to do on a cruise is have sex," he announced. Creative director Steve Simpson packaged that declaration more acceptably, suggesting cruising was really about freedom and escape… "feeling lighter, as if the rules of gravity no longer applied." That led to the tag line: "It's Different Out Here" and a key copy point: "the laws of the land do not apply."

A woman stands in the ocean sensuously eating fruit as words scroll by. "There is no law that says you can't make love at four in the afternoon on a Tuesday…that says you must pack worry along with your baggage…that says

THREE-HOUR LUNCH A sepia-toned commercial for Westin Hotels shows a good-looking guy who "take chances consistently…takes advice cautiously…and takes his tea time seriously," while the narrator wonders: "Who's he sleeping with?"

"CONSTITUTION" Norwegian Cruise Line promised an escape from the laws of everyday life, as shown in the three frames above.

"SHOWER" Norwegian Cruise Line's "What do you need to fall in love again?" ad showed the ship rocking slightly, suggesting sex to many viewers.

"GONNA FLY NOW"
A Royal Caribbean ship
sails into a gorgeous sky
as a *Rocky* instrumental
plays. "You've watched
twenty-two weeks of
football. Better make it
up to her. Before you
get traded."

you must contribute to the GNP every day of your life. The laws of the land do not apply…It's Different Out Here."

"What do you need to fall in love again?" asks a sultry, laid-back spot as a couple share an outdoor shower. "Westerly winds, mahi-mahi with wild rice, blue, blue water…a really nice ship."

Although he had pressed for that approach, Aron found the spots too scalding. So did focus groups. NBC censors ordered that a scene of a woman caressing a man's chest be toned down, and a shot of his hand sliding into her bikini bottom be excised. The sexuality was honed to sensuality. Cruise bookings soared 20 percent. It didn't hurt that a miserable winter plagued the eastern United States. Alas, not even frigid weather could keep this hot spot alive. Norwegian Cruise Line soon killed the ad, as it promised more than cruises could deliver.

In January 1998, a new *Love Boat* TV show had stirred a wake. James Cameron's $200 million epic *Titanic* turned it into a tsunami. Cruising was hot, the Cruise Lines Industry Association had begun telling the world. So, no surprise that a cruise ship would sail in to sponsor the halftime show celebrating Motown's fortieth anniversary. What *was* surprising was its total lack of sex appeal.

Royal Caribbean and Celebrity had recently married and wanted cruises to fill their berths. "To compete in the vacation market against theme parks and resorts instead of just other cruise lines required a big splash," said president and CEO Jack Williams. Royal Caribbean had waded in by positioning its ships as destinations unto themselves back in the 1991 game (see Chapter 4). Its 1998 ads were more ambitious.

THE MAGNETISM OF ANIMALS

Advertising had gone to the dogs and other critters long before 1996. But when the Cowboys defeated the Steelers 27–17 on Super Bowl XXX, it was the advertisers who went ape.

Or more precisely frogs, buzzards, horses, and a penguin (for Bud); cattle (for Ford); lions, elephants, and zebras (Nissan Pathfinder); wolves (Toyota 4Runner); goldfish and coyote (Pepsi); pigs (albeit inert, for the Pork

"CLYDESDALES" Never seen a Clydesdale kick a field goal? Then you missed this commercial from Budweiser during Super Bowl XXX.

"BUZZARDS" A stranded guy thinks it can't get any worse when he collapses, exhausted, at a canyon's edge, only to find it can—buzzards make off with his six-pack of Bud Light.

Producers); a dinosaur (really, its skeleton, for McDonald's); and the (animated) Pink Panther for Owens Corning.

More than a quarter of the fifty-six spots in XXX featured nature's creatures. The popularity of the 1995 movie *Babe,* Coca-Cola's computer-animated polar bears (1993), and Diet Coke's swimming elephants (1995) may have pushed open the barn doors.

Ad land has always been something of a Noah's ark. There's no worrying about multi-culturalism, political correctness, hair and makeup, sordid pasts, or the future possibility of the talent posing nude or punching an umpire. Animals are fun to watch, and because of their innocence, we trust them. Advertisers often turn to them when they've nothing new to say and just want to catch our eye. Nature's creatures some-times function as metaphors to suggest a trait like virility, honesty, or strength, and can deliver mes-sages that could sound ridiculous if said outright.

During Super Bowl XXX, Budweiser showcased two teams of football-playing Clydesdales in a spot from DDB, and frogs with their tongues frozen onto a beer can (see Chapter 5). Two guys in a rickety cabin fend off an assertive penguin gone bonkers over Bud Ice.

In its Super Bowl debut, Owens Corning showed its long-time mascot slaying computer-game representations of heat, cold, and noise to spotlight the

"TATTOO" In a Miller Genuine Draft spot, tough guys in a bar compare tattoos. Max, the dog in the hero's tattoo, comes to life.

"GOLDFISH" "Sparky," the crafty goldfish, plays dead until a boy holds a Pepsi over his tank and he performs tricks. Dad is clueless, though, and flushes the lifeless-looking Sparky away. Later, a much bigger Sparky reappears doing back-flips in a lake for a fisherman with a Pepsi.

soundproofing and weatherproofing attributes of its insulation. "The Pink Panther made our products more accessible and more discussable," said Owens Corning's Jim Schmiedeskamp.

That's animal magnetism at work, Super Bowl–style.

PART THREE

FAST FORWARD

As the 1990s boom
soared toward an almost
universally unforeseen
denouement, high-tech
advertising hit a new
high-water mark, with
chip manufacturers
and business software
giants aiming ads
directly at consumers.

13

TECH TSUNAMI

SOME 780 MILLION VIEWERS in 188 countries, as many as had watched Princess Diana's funeral, tuned in January 25, 1998, to witness the Broncos KO the Packers. Super Bowl XXXII was the third most watched TV program ever. The fifty-eight advertisers that had forked over a record $43,333 per second felt they got their money's worth.

Whether you liked your commercials extravagant as in Pontiac Grand Prix's Wile E. Coyote Road Runner cartoon or simple and sardonic as in FedEx's color bars (see Chapter 11), it was a good day to be a viewer.

A familiar haunt for the Anheuser-Busch, Pepsi, and Visas of the world, XXXII was new ground for foods purveyors Heinz Ketchup and Hormel Chili, and was the apogee of high-tech advertising. Marketers plugged computer chips and software, telecommunications gizmos and services, and satellite TV. Those who flocked to the Tech Bowl aimed to reassure technophobes that their products were consumer-friendly.

IBM, which had dragged its feet on the PC front, had come out with a new computer. Earlier ads used Charlie Chaplin's character from *Modern Times* to humanize the mammoth institution and make its technology less daunting. Now IBM reached

"BUNNY PEOPLE" Intel's "Bunny People" groove to disco while assembling a new Pentium processor.

out to those who wanted to just take the PC out of the box and start typing. In one tale, the "Little Tramp" manages a 1930s factory where lackeys frantically and hopelessly race to keep up with their Sisyphean task of shipping roller skates. Once the manager installs an IBM PC, the factory hums.

CompuServe Corp. joined the 1997 Bowl to shake its image as dowdy stepsister to rival AOL. Things had been looking bleak for CompuServe; then AOL stumbled. It had just begun to sell unlimited access for a flat fee when so many customers signed on that the service buckled. Subscribers couldn't log on and complained that AOL stood for America-Off-Line. CompuServe went for the kill. "Reliability" showed a blank screen and the sound of a phone repeatedly getting a busy signal. Finally, a voice proposes CompuServe "for dependable Internet access," as 1-888-NOT-BUSY flashes on the screen.

Traditionally, Intel ads had addressed only the tech-savvy. But once masses began logging on, Intel aimed to lessen their intimidation. Hence it brought "Bunny People" to the 1997 game to suggest that Intel's improved Pentium MMX chip adds fun to the computer experience. "Clean room" technicians wearing colorfully vivid suits, not the standard sterile white ones, groove to Wild Cherry's 1970s disco hit "Play That Funky Music, White Boy" while assembling the new chip.

"The result was 90 percent instant brand recognition," gloated Dennis Carter, senior vice president of marketing. Intel even sold 500,000 "Bunny People" beanbag dolls. The company followed in 1998 with whodunit ads narrated by Steve Martin, inviting viewers to go online to pick the perp who stole a Pentium II chip from an Intel clean room. A spot early in the game floated clues. A fourth-quarter ad fingered Suzy the Mouse, convicted by 388,761 voters. Days before kickoff in 1999, Intel canceled ads planned to launch its Pentium III because the chip wouldn't be ready until March.

AT A BOARD MEETING IN 1997, Auto-by-Tel CEO Pete Ellis shocked directors by blurting out that he'd just bought time on the Super Bowl. The company's sales were just $5 million and profits were nonexistent. Still, they okayed running "Pain Relief" to illustrate the ease of online car buying, making Auto-by-Tel the first Web advertiser on the Bowl. ABT returned in 1998 with an animated spot in which actor Leonard Nimoy (Mr. Spock from *Star Trek*) narrates a pajama-clad customer's cyber-trip to the company's website.

For Ellis, the ad (which prompted a seventeen-fold increase in site activity) was less important than the surrounding aura. "People forget that Super Bowl is a promotion over three months. In that ninety-day campaign we got all sorts of publicity," he said.

Satellite TV's Primestar Partners first

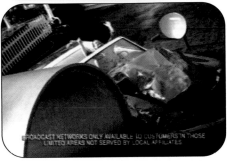

"RUNAWAY PIPE" The Primestar satellite dish: more beloved than his vintage Ford Mustang.

filled the Super Bowl screen in 1990 and returned in 1995 and 1996. A user explains why she subscribes: for the movies, sitcoms, sports, and dramas—ninety-five channels for about $1 a day. "Our strategy was to say it's okay to like TV and really cool to admit it," said ad creator John Peebles. In SB 1998, Primestar shifted from promoting the value of the service to emphasizing emotional reasons to subscribe. A guy is polishing his adored vintage Ford Mustang when a massive sewer pipe rolls off a truck and careens toward him. He frantically moves the car…into the path of the pipe to save his even more beloved satellite dish. "It's that good," the tag line trilled.

Before 1998, the few ads that mammoth Oracle Corp. had run were beamed at companies, not consumers. Then it pioneered a new network, the corporate equivalent of plug and play for consumers. Inspired by Apple's "1984," Oracle's leader, Larry Ellison, decided to see if he could start an Oracle revolution.

A teaser quoted John F. Kennedy and Neil Armstrong about revolution while actor Peter Coyote noted that "history is defined by remarkable

"DOLPHIN" A dolphin swims up to a tourist in Micronesia and asks how he found this secret haunt. The man tells him, Yahoo!, then asks the dolphin where he learned to talk. You know the answer.

moments of change." The scene shifts to a single red chair inside a temple as script inquires: "What's next?" The answer comes in a 60-second epic during the game. The chair sits undisturbed amid the carnage of an Asian street revolution as Coyote announces that the next revolution will not involve violence, but will be about access to information. The tag line: "Oracle. Enabling the Information Age."

Quirky "Do You Yahoo?" ads won yodels when they first appeared in 1996. In an early spot, a luckless fisherman heads home, types "bait" into a Yahoo! search field, and soon reels in 250-pound blue-fin tunas.

The search engine moved to the Super Bowl in 2002 to distinguish itself from the pack. "Image has a lot to do with why people buy one or the other," said Karen Edwards, who was brand management director. "If you have the name brand, people try you first."

Yahoo! wanted more than a name; it wanted a personality as a place where ordinary folks go for extraordinary solutions, to be seen as fun, irreverent, innovative, risk-taking, and decisive—to be seen as the leader. That was an evolution from focusing on search capabilities.

YAHOO! WASN'T THE ONLY ADVERTISER giving speech lessons. The phone companies were, too, although not without hearing a lot of static.

"Is mLife fattening?" Desperate to look different from Cingular, Sprint, and Verizon, AT&T Wireless posed coy, cryptic questions like this in stealth ads leading up to Super Bowl XXXIV (2000) and in four spots on the game itself, never letting on what company was behind them.

In spots early in the game, bickering children playing with frogs describe how they crave mLife, a Japanese grandfather confides a similar yearning, two accountants pretend to know about it to impress a young woman, and a farmer describes how he needs to get an mLife, get to the big city, and "let the pigs feed themselves."

Late in the game, AT&T Wireless revealed its authorship—vaporizing speculation that its buzzword stood for more life, midlife, or a new form of life insurance. Instead, it defined "mLife" as the mobile way to live and connect. In other words, mLife means freedom. People don't need to remain tethered to communicate. Bellybuttons become a metaphor for land-lines.

The company was chided for spending exorbitantly in a tight economy and for ads that were confusingly vague, cutesy, too cerebral for a Super Bowl audience, and perhaps even misleading. Most consumers thought MetLife paid for them. With all that free publicity, *Ad Age* chief Rance Crain argued, MetLife "should sue to force AT&T Wireless to keep running the campaign." (The day before the Super Bowl, MetLife had sued AT&T Wireless to block its "confusingly similar" ads. Subsequently MetLife came to its senses.)

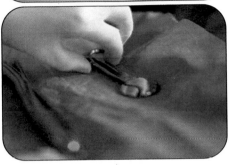

"BELLY BUTTON" In a birth scene the umbilical cord, symbolizing telephone land-lines, is cut. A voice explained: "We were meant to lead a wireless life. Now we truly can. Welcome to mLife. AT&T Wireless."

While many urged cutting the cord on mLife, results argued for a stay of execution. Traffic to the mLife website soared 1,900 percent after the Super Bowl—the biggest jump for any SB advertiser (causing a temporary overload), and 650,000 signed on in the first quarter. This despite the fact that the ads were designed only to stimulate curiosity. (Later spots explained mLife's bells and whistles.)

In 2001, number two carrier Cingular Wireless presented wireless communications as a higher form of "self-expression" and its mobile machines as the path to "unlimited freedom of expression."

But the emotional touchdown was a spot where renowned painter Dan Keplinger, who has cerebral palsy, struggles to paint fiery streaks with a brush attached to headgear. Keplinger attracted agency BBDO's attention

"TOUCHDOWN DANCE SCHOOL"
Unexpected "expressions" come from football players at the "touchdown" ballet class for Cingular Wireless. "You're a peacock, you're a camel...a tree," says the instructor, prodding his gawky students as they galumph to Prokofiev's *Peter and the Wolf.*

after he appeared in *King Gimp,* which won the Oscar for best documentary short in 1999. In distorted speech, accompanied by subtitles, he declares himself to be "unbelievably lucky." The tag: "What do you have to say?"

Qualcomm Corp. also dialed up the Super Bowl in 1998 when the game was played in San Diego's Qualcomm Stadium. Its enigmatic spot meant to suggest that even in uncertain situations, its phones ring true. A man roused from bed by noise stumbles onto his hotel balcony in a third-world country to find a huge crowd below. He doesn't see a dictator holding court from an adjoining balcony, and thinks the throng's excited hail was to celebrate the digital phone he's waving.

Messages from rivals Nokia and AirTouch that year were also foggy, with Drew Carey and Nokia going one-on-one against a ditty-tapping Cadillac.

Traditional phone networks also rang up America on the Bowl. In the 1980s, GTE was the sole telecommunications sponsor, wiring systems for the game and showcasing sportscaster Dick Enberg in commercials. (Even after price forced it off, GTE still distributed seat cushions, which spectators held up to parade their logo.)

In January 1987, vying for a larger share of the then $50 billion long-distance phone market, Sprint used this forum to claim that three out of four people preferred its sound quality to that of conventional AT&T lines. (In 1989, five years after the Bell system broke up, AT&T chimed in at the game. It offered to pay switching charges for those moving to its WATS flat-rate long-distance service. Later research found this the most-recalled but least-liked spot of the game.) In SB XXIV (1990), Sprint unveiled a calling card that relied on a "voiceprint," a voice-activated calling system. Monks chant, a mom summons her son, a baby cries. "There is no sound so beautiful as the human voice," says a narrator before a pin drops next to a receiver.

Peeved by masses defecting to MCI's "Friends and Family" plan, AT&T lashed back. On Super Bowl XXVIII (1994), it touted a 20 percent discount

"LOW RIDER" In Nokia ads, a purple-clad Drew Carey one-ups a purple Cadillac by tapping a ditty on his cell phone.

plan, which attracted more than a million new customers within a year. The following year, MCI counterpunched in SB XXIX with famed psychologist Dr. Joyce Brothers analyzing herself to see why she'd use any plan other than MCI's. AT&T kept the hostility hot in 1996, claiming MCI's claim "just doesn't ring true."

Two years later, AT&T had a change of heart and ad direction. Sensing people's weariness with rancor and discomfort with high tech, AT&T crafted a warm, very human takeoff on the old "Telephone" game.

An ironic postscript: That same year, AT&T sued the NFL for not paying a two-year-old $100,527.18 long-distance phone bill.

Gimp also means a fighting spirit.

"DAN" Some groused that this ad exploited disability for corporate gain. Cingular argued that it celebrated artist Dan Keplinger's triumph over disability and was realistically uplifting.

In 2000—soon to become
a *Götterdämmerung*
for "unique eyeballs,"
"sticky websites," and
IPOs—Internet start-ups
threw away money on
the Super Bowl even
faster than investors had
thrown money at them.

14

THE DOT-COM BOWL

"I'm convinced the end of the dot-com economy came not when Nasdaq nose-dived in March, but at the 2000 Super Bowl. On that afternoon in January, eighty-eight million Americans saw the spotlight shining on the dot-com economy and found it to be bankrupt intellectually, long before it was bankrupt financially."

—Ad legend Jerry Della Femina

ON JANUARY 30, 2000, when the Rams beat the Titans 23–16 in Super Bowl XXXIV, no one was sure who would win until the final play. On the ad field, the outcome was never in doubt.

Seventeen of the thirty-six advertisers were something-dot-coms, and most were Super Bowl virgins hoping to score as Apple had in 1984, or Monster.com in 1999. Many hoped to shake Wall Street by the lapels, to build awareness (and coffers) in a flash, tiding them over until their IPOs.

Unfortunately, many of the companies had neither the requisite creative voltage nor a sustaining business plan. Like nouveau riche party-goers grossly overtipping, many thought just showing up at the grand ball assured A-list status. They figured

MIKE AND MIKE FOUNDERS

MIKE'S NEIGHBOR

"INTERVIEW" Computer.com's intentionally amateurish ads starred the partners and their families explaining how their online store helps computer newbies.

their edgy, irreverent brand of dot-comedy would tickle viewers' fancy—but the ads often didn't reveal enough about their companies or even spark curiosity. And the arrivistes didn't realize that advertising here was just a down payment on a marketing plan that needed continuous cash flow to make an impact.

The coming-out party for the New Economy—some called it "dot-com amateur hour"—confirmed that the climate had changed. While only three dot-coms advertised on Super Bowl 1999, they flooded the airwaves in 2000. (A few, like Angeltips.com and ScreamingMedia, now Pinnacor, saw what was happening and rowed for shore.) The crowded field pushed up the average fare to an unprecedented $2.2 million for 30 seconds (from $1.6 million, or just under $38,889 a second, in 1999). ABC made most pay up front.

Even those marketers who were noticed soon learned one touchdown doesn't win the game. So many dot-coms bought only one spot that they turned the field into an overpopulated, shrill environment. If they desired to announce that they were innovators, being in this game certainly didn't do it, concluded Neil Weintraut of 21st Century Internet Venture Partners. Others thought the odds better at Vegas than in a one-time ad here.

Super Bowl veterans such as Pets.com and Monster.com were recalled better than most. Still, the next day, only 36 percent of viewers could, without prompting, name one dot-com that advertised. A month later, only 17 percent could. In one survey, not one person recalled the ads from AutoTrader.com, Britannica.com, Computer.com, DowJones.com, Epidemic.com, Kforce.com, LifeMinders, Netpliance, OnMoney.com, OurBeginning.com, or Healtheon/WebMD without prompting.

Even with help, few recalled the $1.6 million Epidemic.com spot in which a washroom attendant hands a man $1 instead of a towel after he pees. He also receives a buck instead of a tissue after sneezing in an elevator. The point: You

"NIGHT OF THE LIVING PAPER" The paper monster is vanquished only when the bill payer gets his "money connected at OnMoney.com."

can get paid for something you're doing already—like sending e-mail to a buddy with links to commercial sites. Five months later, Epidemic had expired.

Results were also dismal for Romac, which had just changed its name to Kforce.com to reflect its newly sophisticated "knowledge force" audience. Soon after the game, it crowed that its four $3.7 million spots that day increased website traffic 2,600 percent and memorably implanted the message that Kforce

"ANGRY BRIDES" OurBeginning.com showed brides shoving and scratching each other after their wedding invitations are ruined by a rival company.

had more to offer than job-site boards. A month later only 9 percent of viewers remembered the ads, and its stock price had plunged. Eighteen months later, Kforce.com became simply Kforce Inc. to shed the dot-com connotation.

Even a known brand like Britannica.com stumbled in this treacherous terrain. Celebrities like Francis Ford Coppola looked up stuff on its website and posed questions (Who gets to keep the coin after it's tossed? What do refs do during the week?), but few viewers cared about the answers or recalled the ad. Even fewer called up the website. By November, the company had cut seventy-five jobs.

But the award for hubris goes to Computer.com. Founders Mike Zapolin and Michael J. Ford squandered more than $3 million of the $5.8 million their company received in first-round financing in less time than it takes to soft-boil an egg. (It would have cost more had their agency not accepted some Computer.com stock options as partial payment.) Zapolin, then thirty-two, claimed his only regret was not buying more ad time. His three ads ran on the same day Computer.com's website launched, and the company had not yet sold a single product, let alone turned a profit.

Although Computer.com was more "about seniors and soccer moms," an ad in the Super Bowl would drive traffic, impress Internet peers, lure talent and key strategic partners, grow a company's stock valuation, and prepare potential investors for a possible IPO, Zapolin reasoned. He rejected a dozen proposed agency storyboards to tell his story himself.

Ford and Zapolin initially believed their flash of cash had paid off, and calculated the value of the media coverage at $10 million. "No one had heard of us before. Now we have an international brand," Ford said. "I got a call from every investment bank on Wall Street, and I'm raising money now at ten times what I raised my first round. I mean, so much money that it's ridiculous."

A year later the money spigot had dried up. Computer.com logged off, sending some axed employees home with laptops as severance.

Ameritrade's portal OnMoney.com also ran a spot on its first day in business. It showed a man battling a paper monster that materializes from the blizzard of bills on his desk and threatens to engulf his office.

Nine-month-old OurBeginning.com had a dozen employees, revenues of $1 million, no profits in sight, and was targeting women. Still, thirty-four-year-old founder and CEO Michael Budowski decided that advertising here would "put a turbocharger" in this online wedding stationery company.

"MUHAMMAD ALI" Former world heavyweight champ and current Parkinson's disease sufferer Muhammad Ali shadowboxed against time, which, the ad suggested, WebMD could help reclaim.

He took out loans, traded equity for cash, and later defended his $5 million "catfight" splurge as shortening the company's branding and credibility curve, getting through clients' and investors' doors, and warding off would-be competitors.

In May 2000, even as OurBeginning.com issued a news release declaring the spot a success, its managers had privately concluded otherwise. In December 2001, OurBeginning.com came to an abrupt end.

Netpliance Inc. was in registration for a March IPO when it dressed up firemen, ranchers, the Dallas Cowboys cheerleaders, and a swaddled baby in thick geek glasses to show that its I-Opener Net appliance could make any-one into a "webhead." The ads were as confusing as Netpliance's business plan. The company lost money on each I-Opener it sold, with no reliable way to recoup it. Soon after the game, Netpliance went public. By January 2001, it had abandoned I-Opener to sell hardware and software to companies, and its stock was delisted.

Agillion and MicroStrategy fell into the same trap with commercials so enigmatic that viewers couldn't figure out what was being peddled (or how to pronounce Agillion). As ordinary folks torture Queen's song "We Are the Champions," text reported that "the heart and soul of e-business" sells "a communication tool created for small business." What this tool was remained a mystery.

"CAT HERDERS"
EDS's cat herders
bemoaned the
rigors of the
roundup but
rhapsodized
about the nobility
of their calling
(this page and
opposite).

"SQUIRRELS" The year after "Cat Herders," EDS went from herding felines to running with the squirrels in Pamplona.

Healtheon/WebMD.com also misfired. The brainchild of Netscape visionary Jim Clark, WebMD.com offered a way to link patients, doctors, and insurers. But doctors didn't get on board as expected, the founder was ousted, and the stock price sank.

Electronic Data Systems (EDS) also talked to many more people than could act on its message. Country music twangs as weathered cowboys herd stampeding house cats across the range and river (via computer illusion; cats don't swim), deadpanning about the hardships and rewards of holding together ten thousand half-wild shorthairs. "Being a cat herder is probably the toughest thing I've ever done," one leather-faced catboy confides. On-screen text explains that EDS rides herd on technology to make it go where its clients want it to go.

"CHEETAH" A biker manically outraces a cheetah across an African plain to "Bohemian Rhapsody" and plunges his arm down its throat to retrieve a Mountain Dew the cheetah stole.

Usually one or two advertisers drop an agency after a Super Bowl flop. Six months after XXXIV, nine dot-coms had left their agencies or pulled the plug on television advertising altogether.

For LifeMinders, the break happened days *before* the game. The website had just decided on a 180-degree redirection of their business—to become a B2B marketer. Fallon McElligott didn't think it was ready

"REAL DRAG" "You could be at home sipping lattes in lingerie," enticed Webex's spokes-fatale, RuPaul. "We've got to start meeting like this," he/she added.

for the big game. LifeMinders thought otherwise and produced an intentionally primitive spot in-house. While "Chopsticks" was played on a tinny piano, plain script proudly proclaimed its creation to be "the worst commercial on the Super Bowl." We're no good at advertising, the ad said, but we're great at alerting subscribers to stuff they want to see while avoiding junk mail. The tactic

"WHOOSH" A man reels off what he wants in a car in between shots of AutoTrader.com's pull-down menus. As he becomes more specific (a red sedan with less than 15,000 miles), hundreds of cars whoosh up. He lands the wheels of his dreams and then asks about loans. Whoosh: A thousand loan officers at desks materialize.

seemed to work: 1.2 million new users registered in January and people still remember the "Worst Commercial," but Lifeminders's stock tanked.

Not all dot-com advertisers slunk away red-faced. AutoTrader.com's revenues rose 400 percent in 2000, after the game "gave our business and our brand a much-needed swift kick-in-the-pants, tripling site traffic," said Clark Wood, vice president of marketing. AutoTrader used *Matrix*-like special effects to show viewers how it helps used-car buyers find deals online. Nonetheless, it decided that driving the same road in 2001 would be a waste.

LastMinuteTravel.com took advantage of a last-minute Super Bowl price break to promote its travel bargains. Two crusty cowboys lazing in lawn chairs watch a twister approach and calmly discuss destinations like Barbados and Maui. As the tornado bears down, they make cyber reservations to get there—fast.

"I ENJOY BEING A GIRL" Visa cozied up to the 40 percent of viewers who were women by showcasing a female pole-vaulter, ironically set to Rodgers and Hammerstein's "I Enjoy Being a Girl."

Online-meeting company Webex.com was still going strong a year after it enlisted drag queen RuPaul to remind employees that business meetings are a "real drag" and they should meet online through Webex.

Other companies, such as Oxygen Media and Visa, aimed their ads specifically at women. Oxygen had rebellious infant girls in a maternity ward throw off their pink booties to a rousing rendition of Helen Reddy's 1970s feminist anthem "I Am Woman."

"RINGO" In a spot for brokerage house Charles Schwab, Beatle Ringo Starr belts out a string of financial terms that rhyme with "elation," momentarily perplexing the musicians he's jamming with.

"TURTLE," "SNAKE" A turtle, above, falls in love with Motorola's new Web-enabled mobile phone to Dean Martin's "Everybody Loves Somebody." In another Motorola spot, "Snake," below, a guy uses his wireless to find out if the reptile that just slithered up his pant leg is deadly.

There were, of course, old-economy companies that took to the ad field. BMW introduced its X5 SUV by likening its driving experience to a woman skiing down a steep slope. Gus, the driver of a luxurious Volvo truck, explains that his rig has made him so successful he has a butler! Well-known Irish actors Frank Kelly and Myles Purcell insist on tea at a pub so they can drive the Porsche, and a young girl purposely keeps missing her bus so that daddy can take her to school in his Porsche.

Movie marketers used the game to sell tickets. Six films were pitched on this Super Bowl: *Nutty Professor II, U571, Titan A.E, Mission to Mars, Gladiator,* and *Blade II.* And, of course, ABC promoted its own shows and movies.

In a spot from BBDO, Charles Schwab surprised viewers with unexpected people such as Ringo Starr and traditionally humorless football coach Mike Ditka talking "financialese."

But it was the dot-com dance that people most remember. Their exuberant approach to the Super Bowl reflected the careless attitude of the "new economy" and made for lots of caustic commentary. Bradley Johnson of *Ad Age* noted, "For dot-coms, Super Bowl advertising was efficient—an efficient step toward bankruptcy."

MONEY WAS COMING from *everywhere* in those heady days—and E*Trade Financial was dropping it lavishly. Founded in 1982 to provide online securities-transaction services to brokerages, E*Trade morphed in 1996 into a Web incarnation for individual investors. Everyone had money and was investing it wildly. E*Trade giddily suggested that trading online was so hip, fun, and simple that your biggest worry was having too much.

The politically incorrect rectal humor got viewers to heed E*Trade's challenging concept "that you don't need a broker," said Goodby, Silverstein's Rich Silverstein. "A greater danger was to become a bland brand."

Bland was not part of E*Trade's charter character, as "Wazoo" demonstrated. Nor was E*Trade's other Super Bowl XXXIV spot, also from Goodby, Silverstein & Partners, where two men in a garage clap as a monkey dances and lip-synchs "La Cucaracha." "We just wasted two million bucks. What are you doing with your money?" a voice asked. It was the best liked and most remembered Internet spot of the game.

While the ads worked well, the money that E*Trade had hilariously shown coming out the wazoo had stopped. By Super Bowl XXXV, the bubble had burst.

E*Trade's renegade tongue-in-cheek attitude and chimp remained; its message changed from promoting investing as a sport to warning us to do it wisely. The chimp

"WAZOO" In 2000, Super Bowl halftime sponsor E*Trade Group was the embodiment of the dot-com zeitgeist. One irreverent Bowl ad showed a patient in torment rushed into an ER where the doctor examines his rump and declares, "This man has money coming out the wazoo!" With that, he's rushed to a private room.

"ENTERTAINER" E*Trade's chimp was a Super Bowl repeat performer.

wept as he rode a horse through a dot-com graveyard, past PimentoLoaf.com, a sports car with "DOT COMER" license plates, and a scruffy sock puppet in the dust.

In Super Bowl 2002, the chimp was back in an exuberant Vegas-style musical. In a top hat and sequined coat, he performs some snazzy choreography. But he's been exposed; the camera cuts to a newspaper headline: "Monkey Flops. Silliest Ad in Game History," and our primate is canned and then shot off into space in a rocket as E*Trade's CEO, Costas Cotsakos, congratulates himself for "taking care of that problem."

It created another. Cotsakos looked meaner than Cruella Deville, and E*Trade's message—that it had broadened its services and changed its name to E*Trade Financial to bury any dot-com association—was lost.

HOTJOBS.COM AND MONSTER.COM had nowhere near the marketing budgets of Coke and Pepsi, but their battle was every bit as impassioned.

When the rivalry burst forth on Super Bowl XXXIII (1999), online job boards were a primitive industry, destined to be big…and crowded. To secure itself a lead position, Monster.com turned to the game. The Super Bowl's large audience was one lure, its timing was another, since people often resolve to change their lives at the New Year.

In November 1998, when CEO Jeff Taylor reserved two 30-second spots and a pregame unit for something under $4 million, he didn't yet have a commercial or an idea what one might say. Monster had never advertised on national TV, yet its delicate parody of childhood ambitions, shot in black and white, struck a chord. The number of résumés posted on Monster's website subsequently jumped from 1,500 to 8,500 a day, and employees felt their company was big league.

Meanwhile, HotJobs.com was also taking a flier. CEO Richard Johnson put up his house as collateral on a loan to finance 30 seconds on the game. He'd considered a spot where a man's eye bulges, reacting to what's on the monitor—HotJobs postings, not porn—but instead went for "Elephant." A zoo-

"GRAVITY BALLS," "PARROT" HotJobs.com used a runaway gravity ball to personify job mobility, above. In "Parrot," below, a job seeker isn't insulting her prospective employer by mimicking her every word—it turns out she's landing a job as a court reporter.

keeper is blissfully unaware that the elephant whose cage he's cleaning is backing toward him. Suddenly, the elephant sits on him, making a loud sucking sound, then rises and shambles off. "Still stuck in the same old job?" a voice asks, noting that HotJobs.com has alternatives.

Fox rejected it as tasteless, and Johnson's firm scrambled to replace it. It did—and HotJobs's first ad showed a shabby security guard named Dick fantasizing about his dream job. Thanks to HotJobs, he lands it, becomes a security guard at a swankier place and wears the nametag "Richard." "Log on and find your own damn job," says the rakish tag line. Postgame site traffic increased fivefold, causing the network servers to buckle and Johnson to apologize. Since then he's poured millions into preparing HotJobs' systems for a traffic spike after future games.

"WHEN I GROW UP" Thirteen children dream about the bureaucratic jobs to which they aspire: "to claw my way in middle management," to be "forced into early retirement," "to be a yes-man... to file all day... to have a brown nose." The ad concludes by referring viewers to Monster.com, where the options are better.

Being in the Super Bowl "turned out to be the best investment of my life, but it was hard to call then," Johnson admits. HotJobs was the smallest start-up on the game. "We went from being a little dot-com to being a brand overnight."

So it didn't take arm-twisting to get both companies back for Super Bowls 2000, 2001, and 2002. In 2002 ads for Monster, a woman in a crowd recites lines from Robert Frost's "The Road Not Taken." Others show people happy in life because they're happy at work. To Olympians performing, a narrator notes: "Take away the medals and the clock, the torch, the other athletes and the judges and the uniforms. And what do you have left? … A really fit guy who needs a job."

Meanwhile, HotJobs used The Mamas and The Papas's "Go Where You Wanna Go" as background to a gravity ball from an executive's ball-clacker escaping to a park, suggesting workers can break free of monotonous jobs, too.

In another spot an interviewer asks a job candidate to "tell me about yourself." The job seeker repeats that phrase verbatim. "Excuse me?" the boss asks, and the applicant says that word for word, as well. The pattern continues until the interviewer threatens her with "contempt pursuant to rule 37B1," and we see that the interviewer is a judge seeking a court stenographer. The message: "Find Your Fit."

For both HotJobs and Monster.com, the Super Bowl was that fit.

Super Bowl XXXV was the last game of the pre-terror era. The 2002 Bowl, postponed a week due to September 11, 2001, had advertisers scrambling to reflect a new reality they shared with all America: Misfortune favors the unprepared.

15

THE CALM...
AND THEN THE STORM

IF SUPER BOWL XXXIV was the Dot-Com Bowl, then SB XXXV in 2001 was an endorsement of the old economy. Only three of the seventeen dot-com companies that had advertised a year earlier returned. A few, like Pets.com, weren't even breathing.

But the game sure was—with hype galore. Much of it was lavished on CBS's second *Survivor* series debuting right after the football fest. The ad time was filled with old familiars like Pepsi, Budweiser, Doritos, FedEx, and Visa, and newcomers or relative newbies tickling our funny bones. A spot for Pepcid Complete suggests one use for those now-obsolete antacid tablets made by rivals Tums and Rolaids: grind them up to chalk a football field's gridiron lines. A dad backstage at a loud rock concert finds himself next to an outrageous rocker, "gets" the Satanic environment, and immediately contacts his teen daughters by Verizon Wireless. And as was illustrated in Chapter 6, two men have to dislodge a VW GTI from a treetop after its driver underestimates the engine's power.

Others were sardonic ticklers: E*Trade's monkey riding through a spooky ghost town of dead dot-com businesses mocked the not-so-distant landscape (see Chapter 14). Penn & Teller perform trickery—spinning Teller's head 360 degrees—to demon-

"MONKEY 2" Having established its chimp as a favorite with critics and audiences in 2000, E*Trade let the campaign ride in 2001. Here, the online brokerage's mounted mascot surveys the dusty remnants of abandoned new-economy businesses. A sober new message—"Invest wisely"—reflected the country's altered financial circumstances.

strate that you eat Pizza Hut's stuffed-crust pizza backward. For years, Motel 6 affable spokesman Tom Bodett's promise to "leave the light on for you" has made the chain a hit with frugal travelers who could count on it for a clean, comfortable, cheap room. In Super Bowl 2001, Motel 6 ran the spot it had run for the past year, part of a thirteen-year-old campaign. Bodett toys with the poor calls football referees make by asking one ref wearing thick glasses when he saw the light. As the ref tells him, he tries to pour the creamer in the coffee cup but misses completely. "Well, you gotta call 'em like you see 'em," says Bodett.

Months before Super Bowl 2001, David Letterman offended John Clarke, ad chief at Dr. Pepper, by likening its soda to "sewer water." To assuage Clarke's bruised feelings, CBS offered to subsidize a spot on the game. In it,

"REFS" A vision-impaired ref and the tag line "Call us and see the light for yourself," pitched for Motel 6.

"VIRTUAL SURGERY" Accenture Consulting showed a doctor using virtual technology to operate on a patient halfway across the world.

barrel-chested men in kilts and work boots dance to Celtic music, à la "Lord of the Dance," to promote Diet Dr. Pepper.

Dr. Pepper/7 UP may have paid little for airtime but it paid big-time in harassment. The Humane Society asked it to pull a pregame spot in which a dog appeared to be struck and killed by a can of 7 UP. The Society attended the filming and agreed that no animal had been harmed and even that the dog's tail was wagging after it was bopped by the soda. Still, the Society felt the ad endorsed animal cruelty. (Most animal abusers are young men, a key Super Bowl audience.) CBS even asked 7 UP to note that this was a stunt dog and to warn viewers not to try this on their own pet.

It wasn't all a giggle, of course. In 2001 the GDP was no longer humming and the e-economy was invisible. CBS started out trying to sell fewer advertisers bigger packages, but late in the day went into fire-sale mode.

Accenture Consulting took heat for trying elaborately to distance itself from its accounting parent, Arthur Andersen—a move that, in hindsight, seems prescient. A rookie at the big game, Accenture avoided dialogue and voice-overs to be seen as a global player, said Dick Sinreich, who was creative director at Young & Rubicam. Critics called the 2001 Accenture spot a "fumble" that failed to clarify its purpose. "I don't know who they are, I don't know what they make," one viewer said.

In the midst of a test drive of an expensive Italian sports car that's turning heads at a Roman café, the driver vanishes. He leaves the heretofore confident, now desperate salesman struggling to avoid a high-speed crash. It's a

"PRINCESS" Sarah Ferguson explained what princesses really need to know for Schwab.

metaphor for Internet shopping, as the tag line makes clear: "65 percent of online shoppers abandon the sale before checkout." A second spot, shot in Hong Kong and Paris, shows a doctor operating on a patient half a world away, with the aid of virtual technology. In a third spot, multiplying rabbits represent an explosion in cell-phone usage. Each spot ends with a clipping from a newspaper pointing to a high-tech advance (suggesting that Accenture could help clients capitalize on new developments) and the tag line "Now it gets interesting."

American Legacy Foundation delivered two antismoking messages—one from a hospital patient with throat cancer speaking monotonically through a voice box and the other from a husband lamenting the death of his wife, at forty-six, from smoking. "I never thought of twenty-three as middle-aged," he said somberly. Philip Morris, under an agreement with the government, also warned of the dangers of smoking but directed its message at kids.

Target stores celebrated red-packaged products it sells, like Coke Classic, that mimic its red-based ads. Invesco Funds Group continued its "Masters of the Game" series, which earlier had featured tennis champion Chris Evert and basketball star Bill Russell, with a third spot in which NFL coach Bill Walsh equates knowledge with having an edge over the competition.

In Charles Schwab's pre-kickoff parable from BBDO, an English mum obliges a little girl's request for a bedtime fairy tale, describing how a handsome prince on a white stallion will sweep her off her feet to live happily ever after. But sometimes things don't work out as planned, Mum explains, as the camera reveals she's Sarah Ferguson, the Duchess of York, whose royal marriage dissolved and who has had to fend for herself financially—with Schwab's smart investment advice.

Schwab may have warmed the hearts of viewers, but Subway motivated them. Jared Fogle dropped from 425 pounds to 190 in a year by eating only

Subway turkey sandwiches for lunch and veggie hoagies for dinner. His college newspaper, and then *Men's Health* magazine, wrote up his size-down. Subway's agency's copywriter read it and conceived the "Jared Inspired Me" series. In the Super Bowl spot, Jared is joined by four other formerly fat folks he inspired. Subway's low-fat menu had been available for three years, but scarcely mentioned outside of in-store merchandising. Once Jared, with a goofy half-grin holding the giant jeans he used to wear, personified it, business boomed. Publicis &

"JARED" Jared Fogle lost more than 200 pounds on a diet of Subway sandwiches.

Hal Riney was the original ad agency for Subway; Euro RSCG created the later ads "Friends of Jared" and "Jared Inspired Me."

LEVI'S LEVITY

While launch ads in 1978 and soon thereafter established Levi Strauss & Co.'s Dockers pants, later ones aimed to broaden "user occasions, to be anytime you relax among friends," said Steve Goldstein, who was consumer marketing director for Levi's menswear division. Then, on Super Bowl XXXV in 2001, Levi's unfolded a three-part medical-rescue story for its reissued 569 Jeans.

A disaffected young man rides a small carousel pony at a seedy parade ground. He urges it—in a Swedish accent—to go faster. Next, he's lying unconscious, having fallen off the wooden horse. An emergency medical team descends, and a paramedic discovers "he's a donor!" They phone the hospital with the news. While the doctors scrub, an organ retrieval team hustles a refrigerated cooler labeled "donor material" from a waiting chopper to a wailing ambulance.

It screeches to a stop at a suburban home where a lanky, despondent teen lies in a fetal tuck. As a medic unveils the contents—a pair of Levi's reissued 569s—the boy revives. A picture of the jeans hangs on the sickroom wall. The spot ends on the now-pantless donor, dazed and disoriented.

Levi's tried to win back defectors with the absurd "Make Them Your Own" ads, implying that people value their jeans as much as a human organ. Although

"DONOR MATERIAL" Levi's "Jeans Donor" ad caused controversy but appealed to its target audience—the young.

"CRAZY LEGS" Levi's "Crazy Legs" was the winner over two other ads in an online poll the company conducted prior to game day.

it insisted that the accident not be gruesome or bloody, people in line for a heart or kidney transplant were not amused. Young people—Levi's audience—were.

The next year Levi's asked people to go online to choose which of three spots it should air during SB XXXVI—a guy unwillingly riding a mechanical bull, the trials of women pulling jeans up or down, or "Crazy Legs." Crazy Legs won handily.

As actor Johnny Cervin gyrates down a dusty street in his Levi's "Fly-weights," his legs splay out in a thousand directions. Cervin's breaky, shaky, bizarre leg motions are real, but his ramrod-straight upper body is a trick of the camera. The silliness of his walk telegraphs just how light and comfortable his jeans are.

A year later, Levi's offered a new twist on absurdity. Three guys wearing tight, ill-fitting black dresses discuss golf at a country club party when one notices his wife happily dancing with another man—the only guy at the party wearing pants. Rather than get mad, he goes "slack"-jawed, awed by the cut of his rival's trousers.

EVERY YEAR, HOLLYWOOD trots out ads and trailers for upcoming movies on the Super Bowl. It's been something of a tradition since 1987, when a Mickey Mouse blimp, dubbed *Ear Force One,* visited all fifty states, Snow White, along with the seven dwarves, celebrated her fiftieth birthday by visiting the floor of the New York Stock Exchange, and Disney itself produced the halftime show at SB XXI. Super Bowl XXXV was no exception. Hollywood went over the top with trailers for *Hannibal* and *The Mummy Returns.*

In 2002, violent, high-action flicks *Collateral Damage,* about terrorism, and *The Scorpion King,* starring pro wrestler "The Rock," were featured. After 9/11, the studios had postponed the openings of these movies; now they were taking advantage of the largely male SB audience.

Terror had been an undercurrent in Super Bowl iconography long before the September 11 attack. Movie plots have used the Super Bowl as the setting of a terrorist attack, in the 1977 movie *Black Sunday* and more recently in *The Sum of All Fears,* based on the Tom Clancy novel. The startling realization that America was vulnerable chilled the 2002 Super Bowl and its sponsors. There was also the ailing economy, antsy national mood, paucity of news and new products to launch, and flotilla of other media options.

Starting on January 1, the calendar was packed with bowls, Globes, Cups, and sweeps. And in that year, 2002, the Winter Olympics began just five days after the Super Bowl. No one-day blowout, that was a seventeen-day extravaganza with patriotic overtones (and at $600,000 for 30 seconds, relatively cheap). Corporate America found that easier to swallow.

"It's harder for companies to justify the well-publicized $2 million tab for one in-game moment of glory when investors see sales down or employees see coworkers laid off," said Mark Dowley, chairman and CEO of Interpublic Sports and Entertainment Group. The publicity that is invariably generated by airing on the game suddenly looked a lot less attractive.

However, viewers also looked to marketers who did advertise for cues. Was it okay to laugh again? Had patriotism usurped every other approach? Had America mourned enough? The answers came in ads that were warm, emotional, funny, and sometimes even outrageous. In short, life and the Super Bowl *could* return to normal. In Super Bowl terms, of course, that means the extraordinary—including ads that played as mean-spirited (Quizno's, discussed on the following page), violent, demeaning (a raft of movies), and mystifying (mLife).

Only two spots seemed to capitalize on the tragedy: Budweiser's Clydesdales clopped all the way to New York City from the snowy Midwest; in the shadow of the Statue of Liberty, the horses bowed their heads in respect. Monster.com parent TMP Worldwide bankrolled Rudy Giuliani thanking Americans for their support of his city.

The White House Office of National Drug Control Policy rode the coattails of our national uneasiness, equating illegal drug use with supporting crime and terror. "I helped murder families in Colombia," one teen confides. "I helped kidnap people's dads...kids learn how to kill." At the end of these chilling admissions, the words "Drug money supports terror...If you buy drugs, you might too" fill the screen.

The antitobacco campaign known as Truth, sponsored by the American Legacy Foundation, also jarred viewers. A giant rat staggers out of a New York sewer carrying a sign that the contaminants in cigarettes are much like those in rat poison. In another Truth ad, beachgoers spy an airplane trailing a promotional banner that reads, "What's in cigarette smoke?" A squadron of planes with streamers in tow list offending ingredients. Lorillard Tobacco was so incensed that it threatened to sue. Meanwhile, rival Philip Morris, complying with the law requiring Big Tobacco to spend millions warning children off their product, showed teens angling to avoid the dreaded parental "talk," which, it turns out, is about smoking and drugs, not sex.

Otherwise, it was the expected circus. Animals rode herd for E*Trade (a monkey), Yahoo! (a talking dolphin), and Blockbuster (Carl, a rabbit voiced by James Woods, and Ray, a guinea pig voiced by Jim Belushi).

Quizno's went for the shock treatment. In its first Super Bowl foray, the sandwich chain spoofed its rivals' taste tests. When a plump matron at a focus group must choose between a toasted Quizno's sub and an untoasted sub from another chain, the scurrilous researcher prevents her from reaching for the Quizno's sub by shooting her in the neck with a poisoned blow dart. She slumps unconscious; he tips her into the sandwich she rejected and records into a tape recorder that "the subject dove for the untoasted sub." In another spot, an unscrupulous tester and a glum man stare at a tabletop guillotine. The man timidly inquires what happens if subjects choose the toasted Quiznos sub. The tester releases the blade, and a guillotine slices a plastic hand in half.

And there was music. The GMC Envoy tooled along beautiful back roads as Louis Armstrong rasped "Who's Got the Last Laugh Now?" Led Zeppelin

"DART," "GUILLOTINE" Taste-test spoofs show use of poisoned darts and guillotines to skew test results against Quizno's subs.

tuned up for the Cadillac Escalade. And to put more bite in tax time, H&R Block turned to the Beatles.

It's not just an IRS audit that makes us think of an autopsy without benefit of death: It's the fear of filing. H&R Block knew this, and exploited it just as tax season began. The nation's largest tax-return processor turned to the film-maker brothers Coen to maximize that fear.

In a surrealistic bureaucratic nightmare, a reader drones on about the 441 changes made to this year's tax code to dozens of starch-shirted workers in a cavernous, gray government office. The tedium is palpable: A dry highlighter scrapes across a page; water is slowly trundled out on a metal cart. The point—that now, more than ever, you need expert help—is reinforced by the Beatles' "Tax Man" tune and a voice-over promising that H&R Block "will get you every advantage you deserve."

"TAXMAN" H&R Block's surrealistic 2002 spot stressed the 441 changes made to that year's tax code.

Stars like Kevin Bacon (for a BBDO ad from Visa) were out in force. Mel Gibson hawked *Signs;* Wesley Snipes, *Blade II;* and Vin Diesel, *XXX.* Frankenstein's monster painted the toenails of a guest at the Universal Orlando Resort to suggest how this destination is a "vacation from the ordinary."

Back in Super Bowl 2001, Ringo Starr and Anna Kournikova had twinkled for Charles Schwab & Co. Now home-run champ Hank Aaron and slugger Barry Bonds together delivered Schwab's message to get "retirement advice from somebody you can trust."

And, as usual, some marketers treated this day as any other. For Roche Pharmaceutical, the season was more important than the occasion: It served

"HR KING" As Barry Bonds swats baseballs into the night in an empty park, a small voice urges him to "walk into retirement." It's Hank Aaron in the announcer's booth, whispering over the PA system to incite Bonds to quit before he can break Aaron's home-run record. In 2002, four of the top five spots were for Anheuser-Busch, with Schwab's Barry Bonds commercial the only one in the top five not peddling beer.

up a straight ask-your-doctor, anti-flu commercial for its Tamiflu.

NBC tried to pull viewers away from CBS's game broadcast by starting a special edition of *Fear Factor,* featuring six *Playboy* centerfolds, at the beginning of halftime. "When one network has the Super Bowl, the others tend to just lie down and roll over. I hate lying down," said Jeff Zucker, president of NBC Entertainment.

By the time Pepsi popped onto the Super Bowl in 1989, the Cold War was all but finished. The cola wars, on the other hand, still resembled a largely bipolar struggle for world market hegemony.

16

FOR THOSE
WHO THINK YOUNG

THE PEPSI BRAND had a considerable history behind it long before it first came to the Super Bowl in the late 1980s. In early years, when Pepsi was considered downstairs to Coke's upstairs, Pepsi's ads had aimed to make it classy, to carry it from the kitchen into the living room. In the 1950s, in "Say Pepsi please" and "Be sociable, look smart" campaigns, debonair men in tuxedos toasted women in cocktail dresses with Pepsi in champagne glasses. After Pepsi teamed with BBDO in 1960, the brand began to target a demographic with its own attitudes, styles, and soft drink—the young.

These consumers weren't looking to be effete but to "be alive." They wanted lives apart from their parents and to live them to the fullest. The 1965 campaign "You're in the Pepsi Generation" replaced cocktail attire with surfing gear and other high-energy play clothes.

In 1975, Pepsi took off the gloves with in store blind taste tests against the Real Thing. The Pepsi Challenge worked for nine years, then was yanked for straying too far from its ad mission: "to touch, tickle, dazzle, and delight" and to sell a promise (more than a product) of fun, youth, laughter, and good times, according to Phil Dusenberry, former BBDO chairman.

"ARCHAEOLOGY" In 1985, an archaeology class from the future puzzles over the unknown function of an ancient Coke bottle.

For the rest of the 1980s, the ads focused more on who was drinking Pepsi than on attributes like taste or calories. And they made Pepsi cheeky, suggesting that it, not Coke, was the choice of tomorrow.

In a 1985 spot set in the future, an archeology professor guides his class through what was once a typical suburban home. They drink Pepsi and marvel as he describes a baseball as "a spherical object they used to hurl at each other with great velocity as others looked on," and a guitar as a device that "produced excruciatingly loud noises to which they would gyrate in pain." But when a student scrapes the dirt off an old Coke bottle, the sage is stumped. "What is it, professor?" "I have no idea." "Pepsi, the choice of a new generation," says the voice-over. Rather than make the product the hero, as Coke did, Pepsi made the product-user the hero. Leaving to Coca-Cola the sentimental terrain of nostalgia, Pepsi turned to humor to make friends, open minds, and close sales. "We aimed to be refreshing, non-formulaic, and never hard, loud, sharp,

"GERALDINE FERRARO" One-time vice presidential candidate Geraldine Ferraro talks to her two daughters about the "one choice I'll never regret." Not politics—being a mom. Ferraro never mentioned Diet Pepsi, but it was part of the scene. A male voice at the end adds, "Diet Pepsi... the one-calorie choice of a new generation."

or pushy. That's simply not Pepsi," said Dusenberry. (Neither was stinting on production. Many spots cost so much that the Pepsi folks joked that they gave BBDO an unlimited budget, which the agency somehow managed to exceed.)

Music was a common element in Pepsi's emotional ads that interwove the warm with the wry. So were the sizzling stars, who were weapons on both sides of the cola war. Coke lined up Michael Jordan, New Kids on the Block, Jerry Hall, Paula Abdul, and Elton John; Pepsi countered with Michael Jackson, M.C. Hammer, Lionel Richie, Madonna, Joe Montana, Michael J.

"STREET," "LIONEL RITCHIE" Like the Geraldine Ferraro spot, many memorable moments created by BBDO for Pepsi—Michael Jackson (left), Lionel Ritchie (right), as well as Joe Montana and Dan Marino, and Madonna—didn't appear on the Super Bowl, but for the notoriety they generated, they could have.

"CHIMPS" A despondent researcher (in SB XXIII, 1989) has been typing up her lab report about the deficiencies of her "wonderful companions over the past semester." Her lab subjects, the chimps, showed "poor computer skills, no understanding of tools or decision-making abilities, and a lack of organization." While she frets that if she can't find a missing link, her project will be canceled, the chimps demonstrate all those "missing" skills. They assemble to unlock their cage, snitch coins for the soda machine, climb atop each other to reach it, and leave a Diet Pepsi at her desk to cheer her up. Stunned and overjoyed, she signals thanks, and the seemingly unreachable simian signs back, "You're welcome."

Fox, Billy Crystal, and others. But in 1985, the "star" was a startler—Geraldine Ferraro, sitting with her two daughters in a sunny, airy room, lending her charisma to Diet Pepsi without actually talking about the product.

In fact, Pepsi didn't bubble up at the big game until 1989. When it did, in SB XXIII, Diet Coke was the official soft drink of that year's Bowl *and* sponsor of the halftime show. In one of the first American ads shot in Russia, a dad trying to read a newspaper grumbles in Russian (with English subtitles) about his son's loud music, clothes, and friends. A can of Pepsi sits atop a shortwave radio. Street scenes show young folks skateboarding, break-dancing, and swilling Pepsi while a narrator notes that a lot of refreshing changes have taken place since Pepsi came to the U.S.S.R.

In another 1989 spot, Michael J. Fox creates a robot clone who mimics him and makes off with his Diet Pepsi and his girlfriend as the real, outfoxed Michael tumbles down a garbage chute. In yet another, *Growing Pains* star Kirk Cameron catalogues priceless coins for a museum. A pretty girl asks for change for the Pepsi machine, and the besotted lad forks over valuable coins. When reason returns, he dashes after her, but arrives too late. "Tastes like a million," she says sipping her Pepsi. "Almost," he whispers, sagging against the machine.

IN 1990 (XXIV), Fox returned for a night at the opera. The music makes Fox dozy so he heads for a soda break, gets locked out of the theater, and sneaks back in through a side door, only to find himself onstage for the triumphal Benedictus—drinking his Pepsi.

"LOVE LETTERS" In Super Bowl XXIV (1990), *Wonder Years* star Fred Savage, composing a love letter, finds release from writer's block when he likens his girlfriend to an effervescent Pepsi. "I don't normally pour my heart out. My love will never be quenched."

"SHADY ACRES" In another BBDO spot, cases of Pepsi are mistakenly delivered to a retirement community where the old folks, regular Coke customers, now laugh and boogie. Meanwhile, the normally ebullient frat house crew that received Coke plays bingo.

During the Gulf War in 1991 (XXV), both Coke and Pepsi changed their ad plans at the eleventh hour (see Chapter 4). Luckily, the changes didn't excise Ray Charles in his tuxedo and the "Uh-Huh Girls," in chic and clingy black dresses, belting out "You got the right one, baby" for Diet Pepsi. Viewers lapped up that and nine subsequent spots.

The "Uh-huh" catchphrase was soon ubiquitous. George Bush Sr. used it in a famous debate against Michael Dukakis, and it adorned T-shirts, hats, and boxers. "Uh-Huh" shrank a forty-point gap with Diet Coke to four points, drove volume increases twice as large as the overall category's gains, and created unprecedented awareness. But by 1992 Pepsi's sales had relapsed as if "uh-huh" had never been uttered.

"Uh-Huh" wasn't the only artillery Pepsi fired in 1992: Viewers think that it's model Cindy Crawford who is wowing two boys, when it's Pepsi's new can that leaves them gasping. Then there was "Gotta Have It," the instant-gratification mantra in which celebrities from Shannen Doherty to Yogi Berra suggest new slogans for Pepsi.

"New" remained the magic word for Super Bowl 1993, but it was now about a new product: Crystal Pepsi. Spots directed by Bob Dylan's son Jesse, and set to the Van Halen hit "Right Now," at first look like slow-paced cooking and plant-care shows. Then they reveal they're really pitches for the transparent soda.

"FROZEN TUNDRA" Pepsiphiles in the tundra meet in the ER, their tongues frozen to the soda cans.

Soda commercials have little to say but lots to communicate; they must appeal more to emotions than to reason. Carving out its terrain as young and whimsical (versus "the Real Thing" and all-American), Pepsi belittled Coke's customers as square and feeble. In 1994, chimp A, who swigged Coke, had improved motor skills; chimp B, a Pepsi drinker, escaped from the scientific study to have a blast partying on the beach.

By 1997, the word "choice" had become too connected with the heated abortion debate, so Pepsi canned it. To launch its new Generation Next theme in the big game, BBDO recruited Sparky, a goldfish who "plays dead" to score some Pepsi.

In Super Bowl XXXII, a Gen X-er with multiple body rings spouts Pepsi from where he's been pierced, and an insect-like character (JaggerGnat) modeled on Mick Jagger struts around its new blue can singing the Rolling Stones' "Brown Sugar."

Super Bowl 1998 won Pepsi kudos for its stunt-performing skydiver and an animatronic goose that mimics his daredevil maneuvers. After an inversion and helicopter-type spin, the aerialist pops open a Pepsi, swigs, and then angles the can so that its contents stream out into the goose's waiting beak.

The next year, its sole Super Bowl spot featured *Jerry McGuire* costar Cuba Gooding Jr. as an enthusiastic advocate for the recently launched diet soda, Pepsi One. In the Dot-Com Bowl, Pepsi hawked Mountain Dew, then the third-best-selling take-home soda in America.

By Super Bowl 2001, Pepsi was back touting its titans. It used Gary Kasparov, and it reprised a 1992 spot in which Cindy Crawford had pulled her hot-rod convertible up to a dusty desert gas station and, in cutoff jeans and rippling tank top, knocked back a Pepsi as two kids stared. This time she's a thirsty mom, and the kids watching her chug a Diet Pepsi are her own.

But it was Bob Dole parodying his earnest and famous Viagra commercial that stole the show. Dole, once a presidential hopeful and now a very public

"SUMMER OF LOVE"   Pepsi's "Summer of Love" spot, an advertising extravaganza, celebrated the 25th anniversary of Woodstock. An "irresistible force" causes a farmer to plow his truck through a Pepsi billboard onto an open field, which became the site of the famous music fest. The concertgoers are aging yuppies whose aerobics, BMWs, cell phones, condos, and memory loss are ripe for spoofing. A loudspeaker warns to "stay away from the green pesto sauce. It's a real bummer." Young kids, aghast at the sight of these cavorting oldsters, pray they won't skinny-dip again.

"DINER," "SECURITY CAMERA" With typical feistiness, in 1995, Pepsi showed lonely Coke and Pepsi drivers together at a diner during the holiday season. In a hatchet-burying gesture they swap drinks. But the Coke driver won't give his back! Then, in 1996 (to Hank Williams's "Your Cheatin' Heart"), the store security camera catches the action when a paunchy Coke deliveryman, trying to sneak a Pepsi, accidentally sends cans cascading across the floor.

private citizen, is shown romping on the beach with a golden retriever (the clichéd symbol of middle-aged well-being). Looking like he's about to pitch us a prescription drug, he confides that he's "eager to tell you about a product that put real joy back into my life. It helps me feel youthful, vigorous, and, most importantly, vital again.... What is this amazing product?" Long pause: "My faithful little blue friend." Instead of the sex aid, it's Pepsi.

For Super Bowl 2003, Pepsi put aside the "rug pull" humorous twist to sell nostalgia and glamour. In a 90-second extravaganza, Britney Spears travels through time to re-create Pepsi ads of old. Spears sang "For those who think young" in a 1950s diner, an *American Bandstand* rendition of the early 1960s jingle "Come alive. You're in the Pepsi generation," and a mid-1960s theme: "The taste that beats the others cold. Pepsi pours it on." Other vignettes covered her at the beach, as a 1970s hippie, as a Robert Palmer-cut-out

"TESTIMONIAL" After Bob Dole's testimony evoking the memorable endorsement ad he had done for Viagra, a store employee asks, "Are the revitalizing effects of Pepsi-Cola right for you? Check with your local convenience-store counter clerk." A warning appears on the screen: "Use only as directed."

"TWO MORE KIDS"
Here, BBDO and Cindy are at it again. In a 2001 variation on her 1992 performance at a remote desert filling station, supermodel/supermom Cindy Crawford downs a Diet Pepsi in slow motion, watched this time by her own two toddlers.

"GOOSE" An animatronic goose mimics a skydiver's aerial stunts for Pepsi.

"BASEBALL" In Pepsi's *Field of Dreams* takeoff, a dead father emerges from a cornfield to take after cheap private-label competitors. Dad suggests sharing a cold one, but when his grown son tosses him a "Fred's Choice" cola, the incredulous dad mutters, "I came back for this?" and dissolves while his son feebly explains he saved nine cents on it.

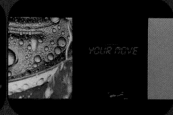

"MAN VERSUS MACHINE" Chess champion Gary Kasparov beat a computer, ranted about so-called intelligent machines, and suffered consequences from the vengeful loser.

"NOW AND THEN" Pop princess Britney Spears drops *Zelig*-like into a 90-second nostalgic tour of classic Pepsi ads—singing 1950s and 1960s jingles, hitting the beach as a 1970s hippie, and being herself in the 21st century.

singing "Simply Irresistible," and as a twenty-first-century pop diva.

For years, Pepsi anchored its marketing plan to the Super Bowl, and previewed the SB spots for bottlers at their annual convention held the week before. More often than not, they had winners. More often than not, they took risks. "To play it safe here would have been the greatest risk of all," said Pepsi's then-marketing chief Brian Swette. In truth, not appearing at all would have been riskier. Despite the nastiness of the battle, the noise generated business. When Pepsi and Coke went at each other hammer and tongs, both increased market share.

Critics and consumers in 2003 claimed to be underwhelmed by the Super Bowl's ads as a whole, yet 87 percent of the audience would remember at least one of them.

17

2003: SHORT OF THE GOALPOSTS

IN 2003, ALTHOUGH more than half of TiVo owners were routinely skipping commercials, more people tuned in to watch Reebok's "office linebacker Terry Tate" tackle and sack inefficient employees at the fictitious Felcher & Sons than to see the tackling and sacking on the field. Overall, more eyes took in Super Bowl XXXVII for the commercials than for the game, according to Brodie Keast, senior vice president of TiVo Service. (Research company ComScore found three of every four women were more interested in the ads.) Even after the Buccaneers left the Raiders in the dust, viewers stayed tuned to see what the advertisers would dish up.

'Tis the pity. Half the sets in America were tuned in hoping for jaw-slackening, mind-boggling, or at least memorable commercials that have become the Super Bowl's hallmark. Sadly, dazzling ads were scarce. Most of the sixty-one spots were flat, silly, boring, or just ordinary. Yet businesses paid extraordinary amounts—$2 million to $2.2 million for each 30-second spot (versus $1.9 million a year earlier)—to air them.

Indeed, consider if what *you* bought in 2003 had increased at the same rate as the prices advertisers have paid for their Super Bowl spots. A pound of center-cut pork chops at 41 cents in 1967 would sell for $21.73, and a gallon of gas would be $17.49 rather than 33 cents a gallon then. A vending-machine soda would set you back $13.25

"SQUIRREL" In a spoof of its classic four-out-of-five-dentists-surveyed-recommend pitch, Trident gum showed why the fifth dentist didn't: A squirrel bit him, prompting a pained NOOOOO roar.

(back then it was a quarter), and a new car $276,236 (compared with $5,212 in 1967). But that's okay—even at minimum wage you'd be earning $74.20 an hour. For all that money and "adticipation," you'd expect spectaculars, not clunkers. Although more than a fourth of 2003's spots used a celebrity, most were takeoffs of existing campaigns rather than new creations. And many tried to squeeze whatever juice they could from their Super Bowl ad-buy with supplemental ads and interactive promotions.

Nearly every part of the game became a marketing opportunity. Schwab named the coin toss and AT&T Wireless the halftime show; RCA sponsored the game's high-definition broadcast.

The drumming began earlier and more earnestly in 2003 than ever before. In December, Trident sent tote bags with a plush toy squirrel, football, chestnuts, gum, and a video-tape of its upcoming Super Bowl spot to key media outlets—and letters to dentists urging them to watch. It also hired guys to dress as squirrels and parade outside the *Today Show* in hopes of snagging free airtime.

"WILLIE" Taking off on Nelson's renowned 1990 run-in with the IRS over $16 million, the country crooner resorts to shilling for a (ficticious) shaving cream in an ad-within-an-ad after he learns he owes $30 million in back taxes. The implication: Willie's woes could have been avoided had he used H&R Block. A sweepstakes pegged to the commercial awarded a lifetime of federal taxes paid, up to $500,000.

In 2002, with its first-ever Super Bowl spot, H&R Block generated record sales and 400 news stories. In 2003, it hired four extra publicists and Willie Nelson to give them something to publicize.

Atoning for not starting early enough in 2002, in 2003, Cadillac hired *two* PR firms to hype its two spots. The "official vehicle" of the Super Bowl and sponsor of the post-game show also awarded a car to the most valuable player.

Monster.com, hoping to top the $3 million in free media it had scored the year before, spent another $200,000 to generate stories. Its 2003 message: that it also serves the blue-collar world.

The hype hose first gushed seriously in 1985 when Apple turned up the jets for "Lemmings." Full-page newspaper ads warned viewers not to take a bathroom break during the fourth quarter. Pressure increased each year. In 2002, Pepsi estimated that it corralled $10 million in free pregame publicity for its Britney Spears saga. In 2003, the hype seemed to swallow the show.

"JACKIE GOES TAG-LESS" Hanes went tag-less but not nag-less. To hype its commercial for its new tag-less T-shirt (where Jackie Chan tries to scratch off an annoying label while Michael Jordan smirks knowingly), Hanes stuffed T-shirts inside press kits distributed weeks before the game.

Pepsi also made noise pitting a present-day Michael Jordan one-on-one against a young Chicago Bulls–era version of himself (via special effects) in a spot for Gatorade.

Eight ads relied on animals. In two spots aiming to identify new Sierra Mist as "refreshing," a baboon seesaws his pal into the polar bear's icy zoo pond to cool off, and a fire hydrant on which a dog has peed fires back a volley of its own.

If Anheuser-Busch "owned" the game, it wasn't just because it ran more spots than anyone else (eleven, including the coveted first ad after kickoff), but because it entertained so well. In one spot for Bud Light (which has more female drinkers than any other light beer), a guy advises his friend to study his girlfriend's mom to see how she'll look in twenty years. Relief at seeing the

"CLOWN" Anheuser-Busch's upside-down clown upset balance.

"STAMPEDE" Levi Strauss went mystical: A sultry young couple stand in an urban street unharmed in a bison stampede.

"THE TRIP" Why is this wealthy American retiree packing his Sony camcorder? Turns out he paid $20 million to be a passenger on a Russian space mission. "When the kids ask where the money went, show them the tape," advises the tag line.

"BRAND ANTHEM," "YAO MING" Besides cute critters, celebrities snared attention. Celine Dion, shot in elegant black-and-white, warbled for a Chrysler Crossfire; for Visa, mammoth NBA Houston Rocket Yao Ming and Yogi Berra struggled with New Yorkers uttering "yo" instead of Yao and Yogi.

"DESERT" What was in the FedEx package? "Oh, fun stuff," says the recipient blithely—a satellite phone, GPS locator, water purifier, fishing rod, seeds—all the castaway would have needed to survive. One fan suggested that they forward the FedEx box "on to the Oakland Raiders team so they could use the cell phone to call for help and the GPS to find the end zone."

"17TH STREET" Cadillac used a dreamy *Twilight Zone*-type train ride to link Caddy's classic models with future classics: today's Escalade, CTS, and XLR.

mom's gorgeous face through the peephole turns to dismay when she waddles in, humongous.

Anheuser-Busch's parade clown who tried to drink a beer and eat a hot dog while walking on his hands crossed the line from hysterical to hokey. Dodge Ram had an even-rockier misfire. A driver accelerates, then suddenly brakes, so his choking passenger can upchuck what's caught in his throat—onto the pickup's windshield. Also unappetizing, though less so: The Quizno's chef so obsessed with sandwich quality that he forgets to put on pants. One fan objected to the Quizno's mistreatment of animals: Their chief chef is so absentminded that his parakeet died.

Not all commercials assaulted with sophomoric humor. A few drew the story out and pulled the viewer in. In a FedEx spoof of the Tom Hanks movie *Cast Away*, a bedraggled FedEx employee marooned for five years on a desert island delivers a package he's protected that whole time.

McDonald's story starred a precocious young boy announcing, "That's why I love that woman" when his mom suggests heading to the Golden Arches after a hard day. And Sony slipped us a mystery: Why is a wealthy American civilian packing his camcorder? The ad reveals that he has paid the Russian space program $20 million for a ride into orbit.

Some advertisers dispensed with charm, though perhaps not intentionally. Subway banked on Jared Fogle fantasizing about a sandwich outlet in his living room. Myfico.com banked on happy homeowners who could get lower mortgage rates if they got their credit score fixed. And the White House Office of National Drug Control Policy banked on fright. A couple learns they'll be young grandparents: Their fourteen-year-old daughter's pregnancy test was positive. "Smoking marijuana impairs your judgment," warns the narrator.

"THE OSBOURNES" Pepsi commanded attention for its Ozzy Osbourne spot from BBDO for Pepsi Twist. The renowned heavy-metal rocker and reality-TV man has a nightmare: As he wrestles with his garbage, his kids, Jack and Kelly, unzip their Pepsi cans to show him Pepsi Twist, then unzip themselves to reveal alter-egos Donny and Marie Osmond. Later, when he rolls over in bed to relate this upsetting vision to Sharon, to his horror he finds Florence Henderson of *The Brady Bunch* in her place. It was the most recalled spot of the game.

"REGGAE" In a Bud Light spot, a reggae guy walking his dog gets around a "no pets" sign at the bar by cleverly passing off his pooch, atop his head, as eye-catching dreadlocks.

"MONKEYS," "HYDRANT" In two similarly themed commercials, Sierra Mist used a baboon (left) and a dog (right) to show what "refreshing" looks like.

"TRUCKER" Monster.com's driverless 18-wheeler rampages across a Midwestern landscape wreaking havoc, while somewhere else an unemployed truck driver leafs through a newspaper looking for a job. If only they'd hooked up before the mayhem!

"BARBERS," "THIRD ARM" A Visa spot, left, featured New York Giants running back Tiki Barber and his twin brother, Ronde, a cornerback for the Buccaneers, to convey the message that while checks aren't universally accepted, the Visa check card is. In "Third Arm," right, another triumph for Bud, a fellow demonstrates to his date the benefits of his third arm.

Nor was there any shortage of rippling muscles, bursting bodices, and explosive pyrotechnics from TV promos and movie trailers. And, of course, there were guerrilla surprises. Diageo PLC, on behalf of its "malternative" Smirnoff Ice, bought time during the game in sixty-five major local markets as an end run around the network's self-imposed ban on hard-liquor ads and exclusive bond with Anheuser-Busch.

Did the ads get through? You bet. Despite the lopsidedness of the game, twenty-four hours after the contest, even as UN inspector Hans Blix was presenting a report on Iraq and the United States teetered on the brink of war, viewers could recall much of what they'd seen. Eighty-seven percent needed no prompting to remember at least one ad, and the average viewer remembered 3.5 of them. The commercials did their jobs.

AND, ONCE AGAIN, THE SUPER BOWL DID ITS JOB. Some of the most memorable advertising ever created has been showcased here. At times the commercials have dazzled us, made us hold our sides from too much laughter, and left us with lumps in our throats. The best have put new businesses on the map or created lasting identities for corporations. The worst have hastened the decline of products or companies. The ads have worked their way into the language and reflected and celebrated American culture. No other event can claim to do that. No wonder it's the Super Bowl of advertising.

INDEX

ABOUT THE AUTHOR

BERNICE KANNER is a marketing expert and the author of *The 100 Best TV Commercials…And Why They Worked,* as well as of *Lies My Parents Told Me, Are You Normal?,* and *Are You Normal About Money?*

She has appeared on dozens of television venues including *The Oprah Winfrey Show,* NBC's *Dateline, The Today Show* with Bryant Gumbel, CNN, and ABC *World News* with Peter Jennings, and has been an on-camera marketing expert for programs such as *CBS Morning News* and ESPN's *Business Times.*

For thirteen years, Bernice Kanner served up an intimate look at the marketing world with her award-winning weekly column, "On Madison Avenue," for *New York Magazine. Forbes Media Guide* praised her "tireless legwork" and stylistic "aplomb," and noted "a Kanner column seldom fails to pique a reader's interest." At *New York Magazine,* senior editor Kanner was also a noted feature writer whose first-person adventures as a cab driver, traffic cop, Tiffany's temp, Wendy's counterman, census taker, Guerlain "nose," and Ritz Carlton concierge, among others, were some of the magazine's most celebrated pieces.

She has been a print, radio, and TV commentator for Bloomberg and has contributed frequently to *The New York Times, New York Daily News, The Sunday Times of London, Parade, Ladies' Home Journal, Self, American Demographics,* and many other publications. Before her stint at *New York Magazine,* Kanner wrote a daily column in the *New York Daily News,* was senior editor at *Advertising Age,* and worked at the J. Walter Thompson ad agency. She is the only three-time winner of the Saatchi and Saatchi Annual Journalism Award.